THE VOICE OF ADOLESCENTS

AUTONOMY FROM THEIR POINT OF VIEW

GLORIA D. FONDREN, PH.D.

authorHOUSE®

AuthorHouse™
1663 Liberty Drive
Bloomington, IN 47403
www.authorhouse.com
Phone: 1-800-839-8640

Published by AuthorHouse 6/20/2013

ISBN: 978-1-4817-6442-1 (sc)
ISBN: 978-1-4817-6443-8 (e)

Library of Congress Control Number: 2013910719

Any people depicted in stock imagery provided by Thinkstock are models, and such images are being used for illustrative purposes only. Certain stock imagery © Thinkstock.

This book is printed on acid-free paper.

ABSTRACT

The purpose of this quantitative study was to examine factors determining adolescents' perceptions of ways they develop autonomy. Although research has been conducted on parents' beliefs about autonomy development, there is a gap in knowledge on adolescents' own beliefs about how they develop autonomy. Furthermore, research is lacking on adolescents' beliefs, views, and whether or not their voice and what they have to say is even considered. This research examined whether a relationship exists between adolescents' perceptions of parental support, parent adolescent communication, and autonomy development; whether adolescent autonomy development can be predicted by their perception of parental support, parent adolescent communication, and the demographic variables of age and gender; and whether there were ethnic group and gender differences in adolescents' perceptions of autonomy development, perception of parental support and parent adolescent communication. The relationship between variables was examined by implementing descriptive statistics, correlations analysis, multiple regression analysis, and MANOVA. Asian, Black, Hispanic, and White participants (n=130), were given the Self Regulation Questionnaire-Academic to measure relative autonomy (RAI), the Perception of Parent Scale to measure parental support, and the Parent Adolescent Communication Scale to measure parent adolescent communication. Results showed that a significant relationship does exist between adolescent perception of parental support, parent adolescent communication, and autonomy development. Race was found to be significantly related to RAI scores. Multiple regression analysis showed that age and gender accounted for only 1% variation in RAI scores. Findings from this study may promote social change by aiding professionals in developing culturally sensitive programs on adolescent development from the adolescents' point of view.

Acknowledgments

Sincere and very special thanks to my family for their patience and support. I am truly grateful for their love and understanding.

TABLE OF CONTENTS

PREFACE

Parents play a vital role in adolescent's development. Yet, parents cannot be present to guide their behavior at all times, particularly when adolescents are outside the home. Parents must then rely on adolescents to inform them of situations they are faced with such as experiences with peers and friends, academic motivation, or lack thereof, and other personal feelings and thoughts.

If given the opportunity, adolescents are able to communicate and express their views on a variety of topics.

Essentially, they should have an opinion on matters that affect their optimal growth and development. If adolescents are able to share their experiences and personal views with parents, it could enhance autonomy development. On the other hand, if no one is willing to hear what adolescents have to say and they are not able to talk openly with parents, this could have a negative impact on their ability to develop autonomy.

CHAPTER 1: INTRODUCTION

Introduction

According to the self-determination theory, people from all cultures share a basic psychological need for autonomy (Ryan & Deci, 2000). Adolescents are faced with critical challenges to develop autonomy and a coherent sense of self. Some of these challenges are developing individuation (Bandura, 2001), developing and maintaining friendships, and managing peer influence (Hallstrom, 2004; Kittmer, 2005). Additional challenges are risk-taking decisions, adherence to rules, dealing with familial situations, and maintaining academic performance (Low & Stocker, 2002; Vansteenkiste, Zhou, Lens, & Soenens, 2004). These challenges tap into adolescent's ability to control and regulate their own behavior while striving to master the environment. Despite the fact that adolescents are able to report on ways they handle these challenges, research exploring how they learn to manage these tasks has been largely unexplored (Chapman, Wall, & Barth, 2004; Garth & Aroni, 2003). Related research has focused on parents' beliefs about what they contribute to their adolescents' independence rather than adolescent's own beliefs (Bumpus, Crouter, & McHale, 2001). Adolescents' voice and input on factors influencing how they learn and thereby contributing to their development is important and they should have an opportunity to express their views.

Parents play a vital role in adolescent's development. Parents cannot be present to guide their behavior at all times, particularly when adolescents are outside the home. Parents must then rely on adolescents to inform them of situations they are faced with such as experiences with peers and friends, academic motivation, or lack thereof, and feelings about social relationships (d'Ailly, 2003). Adolescents are a valuable source of information (Garth & Aroni, 2003; Yamato, 1993). They have rights to opinions and personal beliefs (Melton, 1996). Adolescents are able to communicate and express their opinions and ideas on a variety of topics (Garbarino & Scott, 1992; Hojat, 1997; Stepp, 2000). If adolescents are able to share their experiences and personal views with parents, it could enhance autonomy development and prove beneficial in decision making for the entire family (Melton, 1996). On the other hand, if no one is willing to hear what adolescents have to say and they are not given the opportunity to share their experiences and talk openly with parents this could impact negatively on autonomy development.

The purpose of this study was to explore factors determining adolescents' perceptions of ways they develop autonomy. Factors explored in this study include parental support and expression of views through communication. Views include personal opinions, having voice, sharing life experiences, ideas, and input into family decision making (Bronfenbrenner, 1995; Bumpus et al., 2001; Harter, Waters, Whitesell, & Kastelic, 1998; Hojat, 1997; Melton, 1996; Satir & Whitaker, 2000). For the purpose of this study, parents include the adolescents' natural parents, adoptive parents, stepparents, and legal guardians. It is hypothesized that a positive correlation exists between adolescent perception about parental support, communication, and autonomy development.

Parents perceived by adolescents as supportive and less controlling enhance autonomy development. Parents who are viewed by adolescents as non-supportive and over controlling hinder autonomy development (Caprara et al., 1998; Levesque, Zuehlke, Stanek, & Ryan, 2004; Ryan & Deci, 2000). In addition, parents who provide opportunities and encourage adolescents to communicate their views enhance autonomy (Chapman et al., 2004). Researchers Fincham, Beach, Arias, and Brody (1998) suggested that parents who restrict adolescent's expression of views hinder autonomy development.

Parents are usually the first significant figures all children come in contact with when they are born. Parents are models and set agendas for what children are to learn (Craig & Baucum, 2002). Through observations, children internalize events, experiences, and interactions with their parents (Craig & Baucum). Children's interpretations of these observations are as important to them as it is for their parents (Buddin, 1999; Craig & Baucum). During adolescence, one vehicle through which these interpretations are conveyed is verbal communication with parents (Craig & Baucum). Without support from parents for adolescents to communicate their views, thoughts, and feelings become suppressed resulting in, "loss of voice" (Harter et al., 1998, p. 895), and diminished autonomy (Chapman et al., 2004). For example, parents who are perceived by adolescents as discouraging communication, disapproving, and non- supportive could cause the adolescent to keep quiet and withdraw (Buddin). According to multiple researchers (Caprara, Regalia, & Bandura, 2002; Gilligan, 1993; Harter et al., 1998), withdrawal adversely affects the adolescent's self esteem and ultimately, autonomy.

Adolescence development is a continuous process (Craig & Baucum, 2002). Adolescents are sources of information of their own behaviors and feelings (Garbarino & Scott, 1992). Their ability to give statements of information about events they have witnessed or experienced is an example of autonomous behavior (Caprara et al., 2002; Garbarino, 1995; Garbarino & Scott). Even though adolescents see the world through eyes very different from their parents, what they see and hear is a reality for them. In turn, when parents learn that adolescents do have a comprehensible point of view, even though it is immature compared to the adult perspective (Garbarino & Scott), parents can be better prepared to effectively communicate with all children (Clark & Ladd, 2000). For example, Garbarino and Scott described a case scenario of a 6-year old child who became frightened, yelled, and screamed when he saw his mother in the bathroom with soap suds all over her head. Even after his father came in and pulled the boy out telling him to "be sensible and stop making a fuss" (p.6), the boy continued to yell. A few minutes later, the boy continued to cry and his grandmother took him back in the bathroom explaining to him what was going on. His mother rinsed the soap from her hair and the boy calmed down. The three of them; the boy, mother, and grandmother, talked about how different her hair looked with soap in it. Yet, the boy's father was still upset insisting he was "making a big deal over nothing" (p. 6). Had the father shown patience and taken time to explain like the grandmother, effective communication may have taken place and the father may have better understood that experience from the child's point of view.

Hoff-Ginsberg (1995) contended communication with children involves "entering the child's mind" (p. 78). He described a scenario in which a child solves several problems and in each case, gives a reasonably articulate description of the solution. When given a new type of problem, the child does not seem to have a clue, guesses, gets the problem wrong, and looks miserable. Focusing on the wrong answer, rather than rephrasing or rewording the problem would likely have resulted in the child withdrawing and not communicating at all (Ginsberg). In other words, the more parents encourage self-expression, the more children in general turn to them for guidance and support. The more open the communication between parents and adolescents the more parents can rely upon the adolescents to report their experiences inside and outside the home (Caprara et al., 2002). In contrast, negative feedback or lack of opportunities for verbal communication tend to be inversely related to hostility, externalizing, and internalizing behavior problems in adolescents (Eisenberg et al., 2001). More details are provided in chapter 2.

Ethnicity, culture, and environmental influences such as socioeconomic status (SES) are also factors to consider in whether or not adolescents believe they have their parent's support to express their views about events or personal experiences (Chirkov, Ryan, Kim, & Kaplan, 2003; Conger, Ge, Elder, Lorenz, & Simons, 1994; Dodge, Bates, Pettit, & Zelli, 2000; Spencer & Dupree, 1996). Among ethnic groups, living conditions, family income, beliefs, and values may influence the way adolescents perceive and interpret parental support in developing autonomy. For example, in Black families, parents may not actively encourage independence, particularly for boys, based on beliefs about racism, discrimination, and the importance of maintaining strict behavioral control to avoid behavior problems (Gorman-Smith, Tolan, Henry, & Florsheim, 2000; Smetana, Abernathy, & Harris, 2000). In addition, research on middle class Black families suggested that understanding family processes and developmental transitions is important, particularly because poverty status is itself associated with multiple factors that place adolescents at greater risk for deviance and disrupted parent-adolescent relationships (Gorman-Smith, et al).

Studies suggested that in Chinese families, the "authoritarian and hierarchical dominance of elders and men is backed by moral rules" (Chen, Liu, & Li, 2000, p. 403). Whereas children are encouraged to pledge obedience and reverence to parents, Chinese parents in turn, are responsible for teaching and disciplining their children. Adolescent's autonomy in the form of achievement is linked to family values and reputation. Failure in social and academic performance brings disgrace and shame to parents (Chen et al; Dodge et al., 2000). On the other hand, White parents may emphasize "discontinuity of relationships as a way to promote children's independence" (Rothbaum, Morelli, Pott, & Liu-Constant, 2000a, p. 336). In any case, within a group, strict parental control and non-involvement could be perceived by adolescents as unsupportive and discouraging, thereby, restricting autonomy development. Similar parenting in a different ethnic group may be perceived by adolescents as acceptable, thereby, having no effect on developing autonomy. Nevertheless, adolescent's point of view of these experiences should be considered important and taken seriously (Melton, 1996). All children have rights to an opinion (Melton, 1996) and Chapman et al. (2004), Ginsberg (1997), and Yamamoto (1993) argued that children need opportunities to express their views, thereby, enhancing their autonomy.

In addition to the gap in knowledge about adolescent's own views of how they develop autonomy, there are few studies examining factors such as ethnicity and parent-adolescent communication. This study will add to other research by examining ethnic group differences of adolescent's own beliefs about having parental support to express their personal views on events and experiences in their life. This study further extends other research by including age and gender as factors associated with parental support and autonomy development. This study does so by exploring perceptions of 200 adolescents across four ethnic groups; 50 Asians, 50 Blacks, 50 Hispanics, and 50 Whites. Autonomy will be measured with the Relative Autonomy Index (RAI) of the Self-Regulation Questionnaire-Academic (SRQ-A). The RAI is a subscale of the SRQ-A developed by Grolnick, Ryan, and Deci (1997). The Perception of Parent Scale (POPS) developed by Gronlick, Deci, and Ryan (1991), will be used to assess children's perceptions of the degree to which they believe their parents are autonomy supportive and controlled. Parent-adolescent communication will be measured by the Parent Adolescent Communication Scale (PACS) developed by Barnes and Olson (1982). Details of the methodology will be described in chapter 3. The self-determination theory (SDT) will be used as the major theory in which this study is based. This theory is described in detail in chapter 2.

Background of the Study

Research showed that parents have a great impact on adolescent's autonomous development and their view of perceived control (Caprara et al., 2002; Eisenberg et al., 2001; Grolnick et al., 1991; Tennenbaum & Leaper, 2003). Studies revealed that parents who decide and implement problem solutions themselves without involving the adolescent use behavioral techniques that are highly controlling and that restrict autonomy (Tennebaum & Leaper). In addition, adolescents who lack approval from parents to express their views experience a sense of low self-esteem (Caprara et al.; Harter et al., 1998). For example, a study was conducted testing the hypothesis that perceived self-efficacy to resist peer pressure for high risk activities would facilitate open communication with parents and reduce potential for antisocial conduct (Caprara et al.). The participants were 162 males and 162 females, ages 14 to 18 years old. Results of the study showed that compared to boys, girls had a stronger sense of self regulatory efficacy, but experienced a higher level of parental monitoring of their activities. Boys engaged in more substance abuse and delinquent conduct than did the girls. Open communication with both parents was highly and positively related to parental monitoring and negatively related to delinquent conduct and substance abuse. Perceived self-regulatory efficacy was directly related to engagement in antisocial behavior and substance abuse. The higher the self-regulatory efficacy, the lower the antisocial conduct. Caprara et al. (2002; 1998) asserted the higher children's beliefs in their self-regulatory efficacy, the more openly they talked to their parents about their activities when they were away from home and the less they engaged in antisocial conduct.

In another study, researchers focused solely on parents' beliefs while identifying themes of family relatedness and parenting practices. Rothbaum et al. (2000a) developed specific questions "meaningful to parents across two cultures" (p. 335). The study revealed that among 17 middle class immigrant-Chinese parents and 13 middle class White parents of young children, these parents were less likely to consider their children's desires when making decisions about physical closeness and family relatedness (Rothbaum et al.). Again, research on what is meaningful to children in general remains unexplored. Even minor occurrences that affect all children's lives such as lack of cohesion, family breakups, and divorces (Johnson, 2003), make it essential to examine and understand children's observations and feelings they have formed about their experiences (Garbarino & Scott, 1992). According to multiple researchers ((Chirkov & Ryan, 2001; Deci & Ryan, 1995; Harter, 1998), during adolescence, if significant others (parents) do not validate the adolescent's authentic experiences and support their opinions, they feel compelled to suppress their expressions and the true self goes into hiding. Literature on self-determination suggested that autonomy is essential for all children's growth and well- being in any learning environment (Ryan & Deci, 2000). For example, studies conducted on parental expectations and perceived control in the classroom have shown this to be an important indicator of children's motivation and self- determination (Ryan & Deci). Results from a study revealed that, "this can count for more than 25% of the variance in teacher ratings of children's engagement and disaffection in the classroom" (p. 781). Results from other studies also indicate that parental expectation of their children's math performance did not correlate with the child's self-perception of math (Chirkov et al., 2003; Guay, Senecal, Guathier, & Forrest, 2003). Teachers and parents both play an important role in all children's motivation and academic success. Yet, for adolescents, their expectations for academic success may be different. As a result, the adolescent's internalized view of the parent's involvement may be perceived as too controlling, thereby, restricting autonomy and a sense of self determination (Guay et al; Ryan & Deci). Moreover, adolescent's inability to express these views results in "loss of voice" (Harter et al., 1998, p. 895) and thereby, diminished autonomy.

Additional research on self-determination suggested that certain life experiences present opportunities to develop autonomy, competence, and relatedness which are essential in promoting life satisfaction and well-being (Ryan & Deci, 2000). For example, studies on environmental factors such as socioeconomic status in relation to ethnicity and adolescents also revealed that family SES is a correlate of connectedness and autonomy support (Pinderhughes, Dodge, Bates, Pettit, & Zelli, 2000). Some evidence suggested that parents from higher SES backgrounds express a great deal of warmth and affection and very involved with their adolescents (Conger et al., 1994; Pingerhughes et al.). Similarly, other research suggested that despite financial burdens, parents experiencing economic deprivation associated with low income or poverty also show nurturance in their relationships with adolescents (Gorman-Smith et al., 2000). In addition, among ethnic groups, middle income parents practice different values and beliefs than low income parents. Black parents, for example, are reported to be more vulnerable to race related issues that influence the socialization of their adolescents than White parents (Conger et al; Pinderhughes et al.). Studies on upper income families showed a strong link between parenting practices, particularly in young children's sense of independence, autonomy, and self-direction (Chirkov et al., 2003; d'Ailly, 2003; Mandara & Murray, 2000; Parke, 2000). More details on self-determination and environmental influences are described in chapter 2.

Differences among ethnic group's beliefs and values in other areas associated with autonomy may affect adolescent's views and whether they believe they can express those views to parents. For example, studies in education suggested that Blacks and Hispanics lack strong connection between home and school (Bradley & Corwyn, 2000; Johnson, 2003). According to researchers Bradley and Corwyn (2000), McLoyd (1998), and Parke and Buriel (1997), some parents who devalue education emphasized the notion that it produces no rewards and does not pay off. Researchers Ngo and Malz (1998) believed that for others, striving for an education may increase autonomy. In this case, a positive correlation may exist between adolescent's views of education and autonomy. Without opportunities to express their views, autonomy is diminished.

Past research on families has focused on parent's beliefs rather than adolescents; beliefs about psychological or non-psychological benefit that adolescents derive from closeness (Rothbaum et al., 2000a), parent's beliefs and consideration of adolescent's desires when making decision (Davalos, Chavez, & Guardiola, 2005), and parent's beliefs and understanding of what it means for family members to be independent of one another (Chirkov et al., 2003; Parke & Buriel, 1997). The family is an organic whole and each member functions in ways that complement their separate characteristics (Bowen, 1988; Bronfenbrenner, 1995). Family systems theorists encouraged relationships within the family that also include adolescent's voices (Bowen; Minuchin, 1985). Even though all children continually provide adults with information, in many ways, they are overlooked and are not heard. Yamamoto (1993) contended that, "grown-ups do not talk with their children nor do they listen to them. If we listen to what the children have to say" (p.153) about matters which, in their minds, affects them and their development, "we can better understand the world from the child's point of view" (p.153). Minuchin (1985) and Satir and Whitaker (2000) argued that within families, all children should also have a degree of freedom to express their views, thereby, experiencing independence and autonomy.

Statement of the Problem

The problem this study addressed is that very little is known from adolescent's viewpoints about ways they develop autonomy. This gap in knowledge is even more striking in light of the fact that adolescents have rights to opinions (Melton, 1996) and they do hold beliefs about their own development (Chapman et al., 2004; Hart, 1991a). Ultimately, adolescents need opportunities and support to express their views and thereby, develop greater autonomy. If no one is willing to hear what adolescents have to say, if they are not given the opportunity to express themselves by sharing life experiences and talk openly with parents, then this will impact negatively on autonomy development. Problems such as low self-esteem, limited verbal communication, and social skills deficits are likely to develop. As a result, autonomy development is low placing adolescents at high risk of engaging in behaviors or activities that could lead to juvenile justice system involvement.

Purpose of the Study

The purpose of this study is to examine factors determining adolescent's beliefs about ways they develop autonomy. Variables associated with developing autonomy in this study are adolescents' beliefs about whether parents are supportive or controlling, beliefs about their ability to have voice and communicate with parents, and gender and age differences in beliefs. For the sake of this study, communication and voice include opinions, ideas, personal experiences, and input into family discussions and decisions. This study extends to others by examining adolescent's beliefs across four ethnic groups; Asians, Blacks, Hispanics, and Whites. Details of the study are included in chapter 2. Methodology of the study is included in chapter 3.

Research Questions and Hypotheses

Research Question 1: Is there a relationship between an adolescent's autonomy development and perceptions of parental support and parent-adolescent communication style? It is proposed that there will be a positive correlation between adolescent's autonomy development and perceptions of parental support and parent-adolescent communication style. In other words, the more positive are the perceptions, the greater the autonomy.

Null Hypothesis 1: There will no significant relationship between adolescents' autonomy development as measured by the Relative Autonomy Index (RAI) of the Self-Regulation Questionnaire-Academic (SRQ-A) and the variables of perception of parental support as measured by the Perceptions of Parents Scale (POPS) and adolescent-parent communication as measured by the Parent Adolescent Communication Scale (PACS).

Alternative Hypotheses 1: There is a significant relationship between measures of autonomy development and measures of parental support and communication.

Research Question 2: Can adolescents' autonomy development be predicted by their perceptions of parental support and parent-adolescent communication and demographic variables of age and gender?

Null Hypotheses 2: Perceptions of parental support as measured by the POPS and adolescent-parent communication as measured by the PACS, and the demographic variables of age and gender will not each independently account for a significant portion of the variance in autonomy development as measured by the RAI of the SRQ-A.

Alternative Hypothesis 2: Perceptions of parental support as measured by the POPS and adolescent-parent communication as measured by the PACS and the demographic variables of age and gender will each independently account for a significant portion of the variance in autonomy development as measured by the RAI of the SRQ-A.

Research Question 3: Are there ethnic group and gender differences in adolescents' autonomy development, perceptions of parental support and parent-communication?

Null Hypotheses 3: There are no significant differences in beliefs among ethnic groups and by gender of autonomy development as measured by the RAI of the Self SRQ-A, perceptions of parental support as measured by the POPS and adolescent-parent communication as measured by the PACS.

Alternative Hypotheses 3: There are significant differences in beliefs among ethnic groups and by gender of autonomy development as measures by the RAI of the SRQ-A, perceptions of parental support as measured by the POPS and adolescent-parent communication as measured by the PACS.

Theoretical Framework for this Study

The Self-Determination Theory, developed by Grolnick, Deci, and Ryan (1997), will be the key theory used in this study. It is an approach to "human motivation and personality that uses traditional empirical methods while employing an organismic meta-theory that highlights the importance of humans' evolved inner resources for personality development and behavioral self- regulation" (Ryan, Kuhl, Deci, 1992, p. 702). The focus is investigation of people's inherent growth tendencies and innate psychological needs that are the basis for their self-motivation and personality integration. The inductive aspect of the self-determination theory uses the empirical process and identifies the need for competence (d'Ailly, 2003; Ryan & Deci, 2000; Ryan et al.) relatedness, and autonomy that appear to be essential for facilitating social development and personal well-being (Baumeister & Leary, 1995). Ryan and Deci (2000) believed that based on the self-determination theory, psychological needs are nutrients essential for psychological growth and well-being in every human being.

According to self-determination theory, as the process of internalization functions more fully and effectively, individuals become increasingly autonomous or self-determined (Grolnick et al., 1997). All children's level of autonomy in learning can be gauged from their motivation orientations (Grolnick et al., 1991). This includes two types of motivation; intrinsic and extrinsic. When children are intrinsically motivated, the task is done for the sake of doing it (Ryan & Deci, 2000). Contrarily, when children are extrinsically motivated, the task is done based on the child's needs to respond to parental demands and socially prescribed standards (Grolnick et al., 1997; Ryan et al., 1992). The self-determination theory is explained in detail in chapter 2.

Definition of Terms

Autonomy: is a basic and universal human need for self- initiation, self-endorsement of one's behavior, and regulation of one's core sense of self (Caprara et al., 2002; Chirkov & Ryan, 2001; Ryan & Deci, 2000).

Beliefs: are existing ideas, assumptions, or convictions that a person holds to be true regarding people, concepts, or things (Dilts, 1999; Yero, 2002).

Communication: is a learned skill focusing on how people use messages to generate and convey meanings within and across various contexts, cultures, channels, and media (Morreale, S., Osborn, M., & Pearson, J. (2000).

Control: involves power assertion, restrictiveness, demands, and pressure (Grolnick et al., 1997a; Ryan & Deci, 2000).

Ethnicity: is an aspect of identity based on cultural heritage, nationality, characteristics, race, religion, and language (Atkinson, 2004; Sue & Sue, 2003). Groups used in this study are Asians, Blacks, Hispanics, and Whites. Self-designation of ethnicity is determined by the individual.

Family Systems Theory: emphasizes the family as more than a collection of separate individuals; it is a system, an organic whole whose parts functions in ways that transcends their separate characteristics with family members being open to interact with each other (Minuchin, 1985; Satir & Whitaker, 2000).

Motivation: intrinsic motivation is an innate propensity to explore and master one's internal and external worlds. Extrinsic Motivation is behaving to attain some external reward, to avoid some threat, to gain some recognition by another, or to conform to some extant value (Ryan & Deci, 2000; Ryan et al., 1997).

Parent: an individual who is responsible for the care and supervision of a child and is identified as the child's natural parent, adoptive parent, stepparent, or legal guardian (L. Jones, 2007. Texas Workforce Commission Child Care Services: Section 809.2 (14).

Parental Support: is the degree to which parents value and use techniques such as giving approval, encouragement, independent problem solving, responsiveness, involving children in decision making, choice, and open communication (Caprara et al., 2002; Caprara et al., 1998)

Self-Determination Theory (SDT): is defined as an approach to human motivation and personality that uses traditional empirical methods while employing a structural meta-theory that highlights the importance of humans' evolved inner resources for personality development and behavioral self-regulation (Ryan, Kuhl, & Deci, 1992).

Self-Determination Theory addresses issues such as human needs, values, intrinsic motivation, development, motivation across cultures, individual differences, and psychological well-being (Ryan & Deci, 2000).

Voice: is the innate capacity of self-expression and communication between the self and others when sharing emotions, thoughts, and ideas i.e. "saying what you really think, expressing your true opinion, telling people what you really feel or believe inside" (Harter et al., 1998, p. 892).

Assumptions and Limitations

A number of limitations will exist in this study. The population used will consist of a small number of adolescents and therefore, the generalization of the results may be limited. The age group and grade level also consist of a narrow population range. Ethnic group norms, cultures and lifestyles may have similarities and overlap between these groups affecting the generalization. The study is limited to a population consisting of specific ethnic groups. There were geographic limitations based on where the population is located. Finally, measures or scales other than the ones used in this study may prove as reliable. Therefore, caution should be taken when interpreting the results of this study.

Significance of the Study

This study could provide a better understanding of how adolescents perceive their parents' support as influencing their development, particularly, autonomy. It could serve as a means of bringing attention to the vital need to give adolescents opportunities to express their views on factors contributing to their autonomy development. This could enhance overall communication between parents and adolescents. This study could serve as a valuable tool to improving educational and parenting services for both adolescents and parents. Findings from this study could also contribute to both researchers and practitioners in the area of services provided for parent-child interactions across ethnic groups. Developing more specific individual and family psychotherapy techniques tailored to meet the needs of members requiring those services contribute to the mental health profession. Additionally, this study could create social change that includes increased awareness and prevention of factors that contribute to adolescents' vulnerability to engage in negative behaviors that often lead to juvenile justice system involvement. Finally, this study could lead professionals and public policy makers to design more culturally sensitive programs that create social change more beneficial for adolescents and from adolescents' viewpoints.

This study will examine adolescent's beliefs about whether they have parental support to express their views and thereby leading to greater autonomy development. Factors explored in this study are parental support, communication, ethnicity, gender, and family environment. Participants will include 200 sixth, seventh, and eighth grade students enrolled in two middle schools, both males and females. Participants include Asians, Blacks, Hispanics, and Whites. Multiple measures will be used in this study as detailed in chapter 3. The rationale for this research is that no research has been conducted on adolescents' own beliefs about ways they develop autonomy such as having voice and expressing their views. Adolescents need opportunities and support to express their views, thereby, leading to greater autonomy. Therefore, research is needed from adolescents' point of view. This study explored adolescents' beliefs about whether they have parental support to express their views and opinions. Chapter 2 provides a detailed literature review of this study related the problem, the hypotheses, and research questions. Chapter 3 provides a description of the research design and approach, instrumentation and materials used in the study, methodology, justification for the approach, the population, and sample size.

This study could serve as a tool for professionals to develop and implement programs for adolescents and parents. Clinicians may be encouraged to gather specific information from adolescents while developing goals and treatment plans. Training programs may be developed to improve communication and overall parent child relationships. Implication for social change may include service provider's increased awareness of diversity among adolescents and their parents, and thereby, improving the effectiveness of services offered.

CHAPTER 2: LITERATURE REVIEW

Overview

Chapter 2 includes topics and subtopics related to the literature review conducted for this study. These topics were researched as factors that influence autonomy development. The introduction provides an overview of the chapter. Autonomy, a key variable in this study, is discussed in detail. The Self Determination Theory (SDT) is discussed as the major theory for this study. Mastering the environment is another topic including subtopics such as support for communication, learning and power, and rules as related to autonomy development. The topic, adolescents as sources of information discusses views, opinions, and decision input. Another topic discussed in this chapter is voice and children's rights. Ethnicity is a topic discussing cultural related communication, values, beliefs, autonomy, individuation, and parental control. The final topic in chapter two discusses environmental factors such as SES and stress.

A search of literature for this study was conducted by using psychology databases such as Psyc INFO, Psyc full text Journal articles, and Psyc Abstracts of American Psychological Association (APA). Key words and phrases were used to narrow the search by subject, year, and authors. Web-based electronic ERIC searches were conducted. Online library search and local community and medical libraries were used. Web-based search to the Buros Mental Measurement Yearbook was used to inquire about tests, instruments, scales and inventories as well as telephone calls to copyright publishers. Email inquires were sent to publishers of studies, inventories, and instruments. As a member of the APA, the sources of articles obtained and reviewed for this study were obtained through printed versions of APA professional journals. Maintaining a subscription to several APA journals also provided resources for research. Notes were taken from multiple books. This chapter provides details of the literature review pertaining to this study of children's views on how they develop autonomy.

Introduction

Adolescents struggle with challenges to master environmental and social demands while striving to develop autonomy and a sense of self. The center of the adolescents' development is the family, particularly, parents. The family has a tremendous influence on the kind of people adolescents become and their place in society. Although adolescents' beliefs about events affect their functioning in many ways, a body of knowledge has not yet emerged on what adolescents believe to be factors that affect their development. Therefore, the purpose of this study is to explore adolescents' beliefs about parental support to express their views and thereby, leading to greater autonomy.

Underlying the UN Convention on the Rights of the Child (Article 3, 1989) is the belief that all children should be taken seriously and their views should be heard within the limits of their ability to express themselves (Melton, 1996). Children's rights also focus on holding personal beliefs and expression of those beliefs (Articles 12, 13, & 14). These rights provide opportunities for all children to be brought up with self determination and nurturance, preparing them to live an individual life in society (Melton, 1996; Hart, 1991b). Children are also people and their views as well as those of parents should be taken into consideration in their development (Melton, 1996).

An effective tool for moral development is fostering all children's willingness to take responsibility for good and bad deeds (Kochanska, 2002). Encouraging all children to assume responsibility means in part, giving them responsibility, which in turn means trusting them to rise to the occasion. This sense of responsibility "goes to the heart of moral character" (Damon, 1990, p. 129) and helps all children fulfill the need to feel a sense of mastery over their environment. This mastery stems from a desire for all children to do things for themselves, to be self-determined (Ryan & Deci, 2000), and to learn ways to master physical and social challenges that tap their competence because according to Craig and Baucum (2002), success is a key aspect of all children's development.

The self-determination theory (SDT), a system upon which this study is based, suggested that people from all cultures share basic psychological needs for autonomy, competence, and relatedness (Ryan & Deci, 2000). They believed that when these three needs are fulfilled by individuals and supported by the social contexts, well-being is enhanced. According to Chirkov et al. (2003), when forces block or interfere with the fulfillment of these basic needs, well-being is diminished.

Autonomy can be developed in many ways. Expression of views is one way to develop autonomy (Harter et al., 1998). During adolescence, conflict arise that challenge adolescents' ability to express themselves in socially acceptable ways (Santrock, 1999). Adolescents are pulled in one direction by their need for autonomy and in another direction by their continuing dependence on their parents (Craig & Baucum, 2002). When this happens, they are forced to deal with issues of mastery, competence, and a certain degree of independence. For example, adolescents are faced with environmental and social challenges with friends and the need to compete in situations involving peers (Santrock, 1999). On one hand, when adolescents have little or no opportunities to try things on their own or when they meet constant disapproval from parents during their attempts to develop autonomy, they may give up trying and become passive in their interactions with people and the environment (Craig & Baucum). On the other hand, they suggested that when parents are supportive and provide encouragement for adolescents to express themselves, many of their psychological needs for autonomy and competence are met.

According to family systems theories, within the family, adolescents quickly become active agents, defining and redesigning the family constellation (Bowen, 1988) while striving for growth, significance, and ultimately, autonomy. In each family, an atmosphere develops that characterizes how the family relates to each other (Bowen, 1992). He believed that parental influence is just one element in the larger process of socialization and family constellation. The relationship between parents and adolescents is often the clearest indication of what will constitute the family's way of being and interacting (Satir & Whitaker, 2000). Parents are the models for how adolescents relate to each other and get along with other people. Adolescents may perceive these models as joyful, loving, strict, easy-going, involved, controlling, protective or overprotective, hostile, nurturing, or challenging, as examples (Craig & Baucum, 2002). In any case, adolescent's views about events within the family can affect their ability to develop autonomy.

Adolescents are also valuable sources of information and able to engage in conversations (Nichols, 2005). Parents can rely on them to express their feelings and inform them of their views. However, when adolescents are discouraged from expressing themselves i.e., sharing their views and opinions, they "suppress their voices or hide feelings in a cartography of lies" (Harter et al., 1998, p.893). Furthermore, behavior, social, and emotional problems are likely to arise when adolescents believe they lack parental support to express their views (Kowal, Kramer, Krull, & Crick, 2002). Nicholas (2005) contended that adolescents' beliefs about support to express themselves play a significant role in their development. It is proposed that there will be a positive correlation between adolescents' beliefs about having parental support to express their views and autonomy development, that is, the more positive parental support adolescents receive to express their views, the greater the autonomy.

Ethnicity and culture are also factors to consider in adolescents' beliefs about how they develop autonomy. According to multiple researchers (Rothbaum, Weisz, Pott, Miyake, & Morelli; 2000b), cultures vary on a number of issues involving adolescents and their input into family decisions. They suggested that individuality and uniqueness is de-emphasized in Chinese immigrant cultures with emphasis on interdependence with the family. Likewise, Vansteenkiste et al. (2004) contended that in some cultures, there is little parental interest in the children's expression of views. Yet, Stevenson-Hinde (1998) asserted that in White families, parents are said to involve adolescents in decision-making.

Stevenson-Hinde (1998) asserted that cross-cultural variations also exist in parenting styles. Even though parents want their adolescents to grow into socially mature individuals, they may experience frustration during efforts to discover the best way to accomplish this. Santrock (1999) believed that one technique parents may use is adapting their behavior to the adolescent's based on their developmental maturity. He reported on a study of parenting behavior in 186 cultures around the world, revealed the most common pattern was a warm and controlling style; one that was neither permissive nor restrictive. Santrock reported that the majority of cultures have discovered, over many centuries, a "truth that only recently emerged in the Western world that children's socio-emotional development is best promoted by love and at least some moderate parental control" (p. 232). According to Chen et al. (2000) and Craig and Baucum (2000), parental warmth and affection may constitute a social and emotional resource that allows all children to explore their environment and thereby enhancing the development of feelings of security, confidence, and trust that leads to autonomy.

Researchers Ackerman, Kogos, Youngstrom, Schoff, and Izard (1999) asserted that environmental influences have also been known to affect ethnic groups in different ways. Skowron (2005) also believed the family environment itself has an impact on adolescents' development, that is, the meaning adolescents attach to experiencing a high level of conflict within the family. If adolescents believe they do not have parental support to share what this experience means to them, their voice is suppressed (Harter et al., 1998) and autonomy is diminished (Ryan & Deci, 2000). On the other hand, if adolescents believe they do have parental support to share the meaning of experiences, autonomy and a sense of self is enhanced (Ryan & Deci).

According to multiple researchers (Low & Stocker, 2002; Pedersen & Revenson, 2005; Pinderhughes et al., 2000), within ethnic groups, SES is another environment factor that affects adolescents' development. Gorman-Smith et al., 2000 believed family income is associated with the development of adolescents. Duncan and Brooks-Gunn (1997) reported that an association between low income and adolescents' development appear to be stronger for young children than for adolescents. Even though not all ethnic minority families live in poverty, it is stressful for family members who do share this experience (Pinderhughes et al). For example, adolescents from middle and upper class ethnic backgrounds may have more resources than those from low income backgrounds (Linver, Brooks-Gunn, & Kohen, 2002). Likewise, Winters, Davies, Meyer, and Hightower (2006), suggested that among ethnic groups, values and beliefs are also environmental factors in the way parents relate to their adolescents as well as the way adolescents view the relation. Therefore, environmental conflicts arise within families causing adolescents to struggle with themselves and other members of the family thereby affecting autonomy development (Craig & Baucum, 2002). One proposed research question in this study is does a relationship exist between an adolescent's autonomy development and perceptions of parental support and parent-adolescent communication. The second research question in this study is can autonomy development be predicted by adolescents' perceptions of parental support and parent-adolescent communication and demographic variables of age and gender? The third research question in this study addresses if there are there ethnic group and gender differences in adolescents' autonomy development, perception of parental support and parent-adolescent communication? A review of the literature related to these research questions is discussed in this chapter.

Autonomy

Autonomy is the strong desire to do things for one's self, to master the physical and social environment, and to be competent and successful (Craig & Baucum, 2002). Autonomy is individuation, differentiation, and self-competence (Clark & Ladd, 2000). It is the ability to gain control over one's behavior (Santrock, 1999) and to have one's motivation emerge from internal source of motivation rather than from an external source (Deci & Ryan, 1987). They argued that "autonomy represents an inner endorsement of one's action, that is, the sense that one's action emanate from oneself and are one's own" (p.1025). The ability to attain autonomy and gain control over's one behavior in adolescence is acquired through appropriate adult reaction to the adolescent's desire for control (Santrock, 1999). Parents place reasonable limits on the adolescent's autonomy and instill values and self-control while being careful not to undermine the adolescent's curiosity, initiative, and growing sense of competence (Craig & Bacum, 2002). Real or imagined, this sense of self is a strong motivating force in life (Santrock, 1999). A sense of self allows adolescents to develop goals that fit with their self-images and guide their choices of social behaviors and other activities (Jacobs, Bleeker, & Constantino, 2003). According to Erikson (1982) if adolescents are restrained too much from gaining autonomy, shame and doubt develops.

Erikson's (1982) psychosocial development described individuals as being shaped by the interaction of personal characteristics and social forces. He believed that the resolution of each developmental concept depends on the interaction of individual characteristics and support provided by the social environment. According to Craig and Baucum (2002) and Erikson, the way an adolescent resolves a challenge of each stage involves both the adolescent's competencies and the response of others to his or her successes and failures. Research suggested that when adolescents fail to develop an active, exploratory, self-confident approach to learning, they are made to feel anxious about their need for autonomy and generally learn to deny, minimize, or disguise their needs (Craig & Baucum). For example, a study examined the relationship of both mother and adolescent anxiety disorders to mother behavior in parent-adolescent interactions (Moore, Whaley, & Sigman, 2004). Participants were 68 mother-children/adolescents dyads with children ranging from 7 to 15 years old. Mothers and children/adolescents completed diagnostic evaluations and engaged in conversational tasks. Results showed that mothers of anxious children and adolescents, regardless of their own anxiety, were less warm towards their children and adolescents. Non anxious mothers of anxious children and adolescents were likely to predict disasters. When children and adolescents were anxious, there was a strong tendency for mothers to be overprotective regardless of whether or not the mother herself was anxious. Traits such as overprotection and low warmth were also identified as characteristics of parents with anxiety. They also granted less autonomy. Moore et al suggested that an overprotective parenting style could increase anxiety in children and adolescents and thereby, inhibit development of autonomy and a sense of control.

Erikson (1982) identified the period between 18 months and 3 years as the stage in personality development marking a shift from external control to self-control. He labeled this stage autonomy versus shame and doubt. As children and adolescents become more self- aware, they strive for more autonomy from parents. For example, parents may grant more opportunities for choice and self-expression allowing children and adolescents to assert their desire to do things on their own (Jacobs et al., 2003). On the other hand, Erikson (1982) contended that parents and caregivers who deny these beginning attempts for self-control may lead children and adolescents to feel shame and doubt about the self that may have long term consequences (Erikson, 1980:1982).

Self Determination Theory (SDT)

According to the SDT, a person is autonomous when his or her behaviors are experienced as "willingly enacted and when he or she fully endorses the action in which he or she is engaged based on the values expressed by him or her" (Ryan & Deci, 2000, p. 1025). People have a natural inclination to engage in activities that are self-chosen (Vansteenkiste et al., 2004). As a result, Grolnick et al. (1997b) suggested that people are most autonomous when they act in accord with their authentic interests that are integrated into values and desires. When this does not happen, a person's actions are experienced as controlled by forces that are phenomenally alien to the self or that compel one to behave in specific ways regardless of one's values or interests (Chirkov et al., 2003). In addition, autonomous actions are those that are regulated and endorsed by the self (Grolnick & Ryan, 1987) and are therefore accompanied by a sense of "psychological freedom and volition" (Butzel & Ryan, 1997, p. 50).

The self-determination theory holds that the experience of autonomy and social environments that promote autonomy (e.g., parents, teachers, etc) are crucial for optimal learning, achievement, and mastering the environment (Brown & Ryan, 2007; Chirkov & Ryan, 2001). As primary caregivers, parents play a vital role in all children's autonomy development (Craig & Baucum, 2002). A study was conducted to assess the effects of motivationally relevant conditions and individual differences on emotional experience and performance on a learning task (Grolnick, Benjet, Kurowski, & Apostolers, 1997). The study consisted of ninety one 5th grade children. The directed learning conditions were controlling and non-controlling. A third nondirected condition involved a spontaneous learning context. Both directed sets resulted in greater rote learning compared with the nondirected learning condition. Both the nondirected and the non-controlling directed learning sets also resulted in greater interest and conceptual learning compared with the controlling set because they were more conducive to autonomy or an internal perceived locus of causality. Children in the controlling condition experienced more pressure and demonstrated a greater deterioration and rote learning during an eight-hour day follow-up. Individual differences in children's autonomy for school related activities were measured by the Self-Regulation Questionnaire, a subscale of the SDT developed by Ryan and Connell (1989). Results of the study showed that information acquired under less controlling, more autonomy affording conditions is likely to be actively processed accompanied by interest and a personally relevant experience (Grolnick et al., 1997a). Again, the role of autonomy in learning is essential to adolescents' development. On one hand, if adolescents perceive parents as unsupportive, not involved, and too controlling, they are likely to experience no autonomy. On the other hand, if adolescents perceive parent as supportive, involved, and encouraging, autonomy is likely to be the outcome (Grolnick et al., 1997a). The Perception of Parent Scale (POPS) developed by Grolnick et al., 1991, will be used in this study to assess adolescents' beliefs about parental support in developing autonomy. The POPS is explained in detail in chapter 3.

Mastering the Environment

According to Cook (1993), human beings are inherently motivated to achieve control in their environment relations and that exposure to an unresponsive, uncontrollable environment creates a sense of helplessness.

Adolescence is a time when the pace of adolescents' learning about their social and cultural world accelerates. Craig and Baucum (2002) believed children learn how to handle their feelings, wants, and needs in socially appropriate ways that their family, community, and society at large expect of them. At the same time, they develop a keen and perhaps lasting concept of self. Having a sense of self allows adolescents to develop autonomy in ways that fit with their self-images and guide their choices of social behaviors and other activities (Jacob et al., 2003). During their attempts to master the environment, they must deal with their need for autonomy i.e., "the strong drive to do things for themselves, to master their physical and social environments, to be competent and successful" (Craig & Baucum, p. 350). Yet, Bradley and Corwyn (2000), argued that due to of the large number of potential influences on development, conflicts arise causing adolescents to adjust to changes and forces them to deal with issues of mastery and competence.

Attachments theorists Ainsworth (1989) Ainsworth and Marvin (1995), and Bowlby (1989), emphasized the importance of connectedness and autonomy support in the parent-adolescent relationship. It is viewed as a motivating force driving development and the necessity of the adolescent's individuation from the parent (Clark & Ladd, 2000). According to multiple researchers (Baumesiter & Leary, 1995; Goldberg, Grusec, & Jenkins, 1999), during infancy, the attachment system encompasses behaviors and emotional states relevant to infant signals that elicit protection from mothers and fathers whose roles both impact on the child's development. Braungart-Rieker, Garwood, Powers, and Notaro (1999) conducted a study examining the association among family type (single-earner vs. dual earner families of sons and daughters), parent sensitivity, marital adjustment, infant emotionality, infant-mother attachment, and infant-father attachment. Participants included 77 families who were observed in a laboratory at 4, 12, and 13 months. Results indicated that infant-father but not infant-mother attachment was related to family type such as father-son, but not father-daughter. In contrast, infant-mother attachment security was not associated with family type. Furthermore, infant boys and girls were more negatively emotional at 4 months towards fathers. Yet, boys were more negatively emotional than were girls at 4 months (Braugart et al.). Thus, each family member is part of a multiple system (Satir & Whitaker, 2000) and each system can impact each other as well as the child's development.

Beginning in infancy, a person's sense of control over the environment is a psychological significance (Cook, 1993). According to Bowlby (1989), the infant's confidence that the caregiver will be protective enables the infant to begin to master the environment by exploring the world and learning new skills. Even though the content of self-beliefs during infancy is generally positive, differences have been linked to parents' level of responsiveness and support (Jacobs et al., 2003). For example, research suggested that securely attached adolescents who have experienced responsive care giving develop a working model of the self as being effective (Bohlin, Hagekull, & Anderson, 2005). Contrarily, adolescents whose parents are inconsistently available develop models of self that can be described as ineffective and uncertain. Finally, adolescents whose parents have exhibited little warmth but high control develop working models in which the self is unworthy and lacks competence (Bohlin et al., 2005). A longitudinal study was conducted to test the hypothesis that secure attachment promotes later social competence (Bohlin et al., 2000). Ninety-six children were followed from 15 months to ages 8-9 years. Attachment relationships were studied in infancy with the Strange Situation and at school age with the Separation Anxiety Test. Social functioning was studied at school age through mother and teacher ratings, observations at school, and in children's self reports. Predictive results showed that infants who had been secure as infants were more socially active, positive, and popular at school age, and tended to report less social anxiety than children who had been insecure. Attachment security is associated with good social functioning during childhood and adolescent age (Bohlin et al., 2000). Past research conducted by Moss, Cyr, and Dubois-Comtois (2004), supported the view that the secure child can be self-reliant while openly communicating emotions and needs necessary to negotiate interpersonal difficulties.

Support for Communication

According to Cook (1993), beginning in childhood, parent-child relationships are believed to play a central role in the early development sense of control that leads to autonomy. Attachment theorists, Ainsworth and Marvin (1995), predicted that parent-child dyads that were securely attached in infancy would exhibit emotionally open, fluent, and coherent verbal communication. Researchers Sales, Milhhausen, Wingood, DiClemente, Salazar, and Crosby (2006) contended that a hallmark of secure attachment is open and relaxed communication between parent and child, particularly with regard to communication. For example, a study with 68 children, 32 male and 36 female ages 4.5 to 6.75 was conducted to examine mother's scaffolding (an instructional interaction aimed at extending the child's knowledge, reducing task complexity, and transferring responsibility while providing emotional support) and children's academic self regulatory behaviors in school (Neitzel & Stright, 2003). Results showed that meta-cognitive content and manner of instruction were predictors of child behaviors related to awareness and management. Emotional support and transfer of responsibility were related to children's task persistence and behavior control in school. Thus, mother's scaffolding lays a foundation for children's subsequent academic self regulatory competence. As a result, during adolescence, they develop abilities to self regulate from interactions overseen by parents in supportive settings that are abundant in communication (Nietzel & Stright). Similarly, sensitive and responsive parents who promote adolescents' beliefs that they can exercise control over their life events can teach adolescents a sense of self-efficacy (Bandura, 1990; Caprara, Regalia, Scabini, Barbarnelli, & Bandura, 2004). However, Cook argued that adolescents whose parents overprotect them may not feel they can influence the world around them.

Furthermore, children with generally responsive and supportive parents develop autonomy and learn ways to meet social goals during adolescence (Clark & Ladd, 2000; Goldberg et al, 1999). For example, a study of 192 five year olds and their mothers was conducted to examine relation in children's relational competence, including socio emotional orientations, friendships, and peers acceptance (Clark & Ladd). Results showed that connectedness was correlated with children's socio emotional orientations, number of mutual friendships, and peer acceptance and that relation between parent-child connectedness and children's peer relationships was mediated by children's pro-social empathic orientations leading to autonomy (Clark & Ladd). He suggested that the type of parent-child talk that seems optimal for inferring qualities of later parent-adolescent relationship is "personal narrative conversation about the child's experience" (p. 487).

Moreover, the process by which a parent and adolescents discuss their experiences may shape the adolescents' incorporation of the experience into his or her self-development (Landry, Smith, & Swank, 2006; Levine, Stein, & Liwag, 1999). Parents who support adolescents when they tell about life experiences and respond with interest convey to adolescents that they are capable of worthwhile insights and feelings. Subsequently, this type of interaction enhances autonomy (Brown & Ryan, 2007; Clark & Ladd, 2000). However, no studies have been conducted examining the adolescent's point of view. This study will add to previous research by examining adolescents' beliefs about whether they have parental support to express their experiences and viewpoints.

The transition from childhood to adolescence present special challenges in the way adolescents manage social roles with growing independence (Eccles, Early, Frasier, Belansky, & McCarthy, 1996). Whereas parents continue to serve as an important source of guidance, support and trust (Scabini, Lanz, Marta, 1999), the more they encourage personal expression of personal preferences and the more open the communication between parents and adolescents, the more parents can rely upon their adolescents to report on activities outside the home and dissuade from activities that would be disapproved by their parents (Caprara et al., 2002). A longitudinal study was conducted to examine the impact of self-efficacy and parental communication on violent conduct. The participants were 350 adolescents, 170 boys and 180 girls, with a mean age of 16 years in the initial phase and 18 years in the subsequent phase of the longitudinal study. A 10-item subscale from the 20-item PACS developed by Barnes and Olson (1982) was used to assess adolescent's open and problematic communication. The adolescents rated on the 5-point scale, the extent to which they felt free to discuss problems with their parents and that they would respond in an understanding, supportive way. Results of the study showed that compared to boys, girls had a stronger sense of self-efficacy and reported better communication with their mothers than fathers. Boys engaged in more violent activities than did girls. Perceived self-regulatory efficacy contributed to violent conduct concurrently and longitudinally after controlling for prior levels of violent conduct and openness of parental communication (Caprara et al.). They believed the quality of familial communication can make a difference in the way adolescents manage situations outside the home and thereby, affecting autonomy. This study will build on previous research by using the PACS with four ethnic groups of adolescents to assess beliefs about whether they can openly communicate with parents. The PACS is described in detail in Chapter 3 of this study.

Researchers Caprara et al.(1998) and d'Ailly (2003) asserted that the relationship between parents and adolescents are factors in the emergence of self-regulatory skills, linguistic abilities, and developing autonomy. Self-regulation involves self-monitoring, efforts, feelings, and behaviors to reach a goal. According to the self-determination theory, all children's level of autonomy in learning can be gauged from motivation orientations (Ryan & Deci, 2000). The theory suggested that when children are internally motivated, they explore and master their world for the sake of inherent satisfaction (Grolnick et al., 1997). In contrast, external motivation is "based on one's need to respond to socially prescribed demands, limits, and patterns of behavior to avoid some threat or to conform to some extant value" (Ryan et al., 1992, p. 170). A model of motivation and achievement was tested during a study of 50 teachers and 806 students, grades 4-6 in Taiwan (d'Ailly). Data was collected using the Children's Perception of Parents Scale by (Grolnick et al, 1991), the Student's Perception of Control Questionnaire: Academic Domain by Wellborn, Connell, and Skinner, (1989), and the Self-Regulation Questionnaire Academic by Ryan & Connell, (1989). The SRQ-A is a subscale used by the Self Determination Theory. Results showed that maternal involvement and autonomy support, as well as teachers' autonomy support are important for children's autonomy and perceived control (d'Ailly). Therefore, parents and teachers who contribute to developing patterns of self-regulation in children promote autonomy. According to multiple researchers (Bandura; 1997; Brown & Ryan, 2007; Capara et al., 2002; Grotevant & Cooper, 1998), parents who encourage self-regulatory learning in children teach self-regulatory and responsible behavior in adolescents.

Researchers Capara et al. (2004) suggested that a family is a social system that exerts an ongoing influence on human development. The different roles of spouses, parent, and adolescents carry different opportunities, constraints, and reciprocal obligations. Every role represents an "aspect of life and those role requirements may prove critical for individuals and family functioning" (p. 248). They conducted a study with a sample of 600 parents and 1000 adolescents from a community near Rome and Milan, Italy. Families included skilled workers, professionals, merchants, and service staff. Adolescents' perceived self-efficacy was measured with 20 items, 5 point scale PACS developed by Barnes and Olson (1982). This included two dimensions; Openness and Problems. Results showed that for adolescents both perceived filial self-efficacy and prescribed family efficacy were significantly related to family functioning variables (Caprara et al.). This was evidenced by the pattern of positive correlations between efficacy beliefs and dimensions of positive family functioning and negative correlations between efficacy beliefs and dimensions of poor family functioning. For adolescents, parents demonstrated a similar pattern of correlations with family efficacy beliefs showing higher positive correlations with satisfaction, open communication. However, for fathers, beliefs about family efficacy were more highly negatively correlated with communication problems and aggressive management conflicts than for mothers (Caprara et al., 2004). They believed the more confident adolescents are in their filial and collective family efficacy, the more likely they are to comply with monitoring and turn to parents for support. This type of encouragement enhances adolescents' autonomy.

Learning and Power

Social learning theorists such as Bandura (1986) believed that people learn by observing what others do. Through observational learning, people cognitively interpret the behavior of others and possibly adopt this behavior themselves. Bandura's (1997) summarized the model of learning and development as involving behavior, the person, and the environment (Bandura). Likewise, Damon (1990) believed that observation is a valuable key to understanding adolescents' behavioral response based on their perceptions and interpretations. Observing is a human process involving both the observer and the observed (Bandura, 1997). The assumptions and beliefs of the observer influences the quality and quantity of the information gathered. There are also distinct advantages associated with the process of observation. Garbarino and Scott (1992) suggested that one advantage of the observation process is that humans are usually sensitive and receptive, thereby, adding a unique dimension of depth to the quality of information obtained. Through adolescents' observation, therefore, they provide adults with information. Adults need to listen and recognize significant clues because some of these clues reflect where the child is developmentally (Stepp, 2000). He believed that observation is a natural method both adults and adolescents can use to collect information about each other.

Social learning theories believed adolescents first learn about social power during early relationships with their parents. These interactions provide a prototypical example of power-based relationships. These relationships are influenced by the unequal power or control that is present between parents and adolescents. Subsequently, adolescents respond to other adults in ways that are influenced by their understanding of the relationship with parents (Caprara et al., 2004; d'Ailly, 2003). For example, adolescents who have a low perceived balance of power or who attribute much more power or control to parents than to themselves are highly reactive to potential threat from other adults. According to multiple researchers (Silk, Morris, Kanaga, & Steinberg, 2003), they react with higher levels of avoidance and processing deficits when confronted by a threatening adult. To illustrate, a study was conducted examining children's views of authority interactions with 144 children and adolescents, ages 6 to 11 years of age. Vignettes describing everyday conflicts between children, adolescents, adult authorities (parent, teacher, police lifeguard, store manager, and librarian) were used (Braine, Pomerantz, Lorber, & Krantz, 1997). Results revealed that children and adolescents were reported as feeling bad, as complying, and as anticipating negative consequences for noncompliance. There was a positive correlation between compliance and the anticipation of negative consequences. Although both children and adolescents saw the authority interactions as coercive, their justifications did not refer primarily to coercion. Rather, "they viewed authority relations as involving an interplay between coercion and legitimate reasons for compliance" (p. 832). Again, control and power can be viewed by children and adolescents as threatening (Silk et al.) and coercive (Braine et al.) which are both factors in their development.

Another study conducted by Han, Weisz, and Mesman (2001), examined the specificity of the relation between 3 types of control related beliefs and internalizing and externalizing psychopathology was conducted on 290 clinic referred children and adolescents ages 7 to 17. The self reported belief about control was the capacity to cause an intended outcome. Contingency was the degree to which a desire to outcome can be controlled by a relevant behavior, and competence; an individual's ability to produce the relevant behavior across three domains; academic, behavioral, and social (Han et al.). According to Bandura (1997), the beliefs in one's capacity to cause a desired effect and interactions with people and other aspects of one's environment is a necessary element in the initiation and consistency of goal directed behavior. Ryan and Deci (2000) believed this process has received strong confirmation with perceptions of personal control being linked to motivation, persistence, task performance and academic achievement (Hans et al., 2001) and planning in problem-solving behaviors (Landry et al., 2006). Results of the study showed that among children and adolescents with externalizing psychopathology, internalized psychopathology may be specifically associated with increased self-critical awareness about their conduct (Hans et al). They suggested that children and adolescent's perceptions of parental control may result in behavior problems adversely affecting autonomy.

Rules

According to Satir (1988), based on the family systems theory, children enter into families that are already loaded with rules. As they grow becoming adolescents, more rules are developed to aid the family in functioning properly. Multiple researchers (Blake, Simkin, Ledsky, Perkins, & Calabrese, 2001), suggested that the most important rules are ones that govern communication; who says what to whom and under what conditions. In healthy families, depending on situations, rules are realistic, relevant, consistently applied, and flexible (Satir, 1994). Family rules govern individuation and sharing information in the form of communication. These rules influence the ability of a family member to function openly allowing all members the possibility to change. In contrast, an unhealthy family is characterized by closed communication and rigid patterns of behavior. This kind of family resists awareness, is unresponsive, and there is little support for individuality. In this type of environment, Blake et al. believed that autonomous support does not exist among family members.

Furthermore, rules may be spoken or unspoken and are embedded in the behavioral responses and interactions of the family system. Rules are intended to provide a safety net for all children as they venture into the world (Satir & Bitter, 2000; Bronfenbrenner, 1998). A longitudinal study was conducted examining how 71 mothers socialize their young children toward behavioral self regulation (Gralinski & Kopp, 1993). Thirty three were mothers of younger children and 38 were mothers of older children. Mothers and children were recruited from local toddler or nursery programs. Mothers were presented with open ended questionnaires about things they insist on or encourage their children to try. Results showed (a) commonalities among mothers in the network of rules being socialized (b), age related increases in numbers and kinds of rules and (c) a shift in the structure of rule networks from an early emphasis on safety toward encouraging autonomy and integrating children into the family. For children, findings revealed (a) compliance was highest in situations that involved rules for safety and other's possessions and (b) gradual age related movement from external control to internally mediated compliance (Gralinski & Kopp). Thus, these researchers suggest that the role of parents is multifaceted and includes decisions about specific rules and standards of behaviors that "ought be communicated to young children, when they should be communicated" (p. 573) at an early age. They believed this increases their understanding and aids internalization. Likewise, Caprara et al. (1998) suggested that open familial communication provides opportunities for parents to provide guidance and safeguard against children's involvement in risky activities.

Adolescents also learn rules by observing the behavior of their parents. According to multiple researchers (Fincham et al., 1998; Neiderhiser, Pike, Hetherton, & Reiss, 1998), when rules are presented as absolutes without choice and parental behaviors are inconsistent with rules conveyed, they typically pose problems for adolescents. A study was conducted by Fincham et al. to assess adolescent's attribution in parent-adolescent relationships, examined if an association between behavior displayed toward the parent and depressed symptoms were linked. The study consisted on 232 adolescents (116 girls and 116 boys) with married parents. Their ages ranged from 10 to 12 years old. The adolescents were recruited from 12 non-metropolitan counties in Georgia. The Children's Relationship Attribution Measure was used to assess adolescent's attribution of parental behaviors. It was hypothesized that attributions accentuating the impact of negative parent behavior would be positively related to reports of maladaptive conduct interactions and positively related to the behavior observed in parent-adolescent interactions. Results showed that adolescents' attribution for parent behaviors were, "positively related to the parent-adolescent relationship and to self and parent reported conflict, and observed behavior with the father" (p. 481). The associations were not found to be due to depressive symptoms. The results underscored the importance of adolescents' perceptions of family processes. Just as the attribution processes have proven to be important in understanding adult relationships, adolescent's feelings about and behavior toward their parents are helpful in understanding their responses to family events (Fincham et al.). Adolescents' views of family processes provide a window on how adolescents make sense of an important aspect of their interpersonal world. This study expands previous research by adding adolescents' views as opposed to parents.

Erikson (1982) contended that gradual and well guided experience of free choice will contribute to the adolescent's autonomy whereas over control is likely to result in opposite outcome. According to Fosco and Grych (2007), adolescents are most likely to comply if they perceive that they are participating in a reciprocal relationship, that is, the adolescent is willing to accept the influence attempt of the parent if the parent has accepted influence attempt of the adolescent. They argued the more open the communication between parents and adolescents, the greater the consensus on reciprocal interactions.

According to Choo (2002), children in other countries provide insightful information about their perceptions of parent child relationships. He conducted with 748 Singapore adolescents, ages 16-19 years old, on their perception of their parents' child rearing behaviors and the relationship to the adolescent's psychosocial adjustment and autonomy development. The study assessed three parenting behaviors; warmth, control, and communication. The PACS developed by Barnes and Olson (1982) was used to measure openness in communication with father/mother and the quality of affect in the parent-child communication. Findings revealed that adolescents perceived mothers to be the more nurturing and supportive parent. Fathers and mothers' parenting behaviors were linked to all measures of psychosocial competence and adjustment, with stronger associations with mother's parenting behaviors (Choo). He suggested that parental control is linked to psychosocial adjustment, suggesting that adolescents may interpret negatively any parental attempt to limit their autonomy, a very important aspect of psychosocial development in adolescent.

According to Soenens, Vansteenkiste, Luyckx, & Goossens (2006), key variables that facilitate autonomy, self-regulation, and mediate the transmission of rules and standards from parents to adolescents are parental warmth, sensitivity, responsiveness, and open communication. Garbarino (1992) asserted that when parents communicate with their adolescents, they ask questions that are rhetorical and not used to elicit information. He believed that parents usually expect agreement or behavior compliance from adolescents, not information, suggesting that adolescents are to be seen but not heard. Contrarily, family system theorists, Satir (1988) and Whitaker (1992), suggested the family should be characterized by freedom, flexibility, and open communication. They believed that all the members within the family hold a voice and can speak for themselves. In this atmosphere, individuals feel support for taking risk and venturing into the world. A healthy family encourages sharing experiences; the members are secure enough to be themselves and to allow others to be whom they are (Satir; Whitaker). According to Satir, each member is allowed to have a separate life as well as a shared life with the family. Different relationships are welcomed and nurtured. Change is expected and invited, rather than viewed as a threat. When differences lead to disagreements, the situation is viewed as an opportunity for growth rather than an attack on the family system (Satir & Whitaker, 2000). Parents are encouraged to listen and accept adolescents' views as well as their needs. Likewise, Brannen (2002) and Soto, Levenson, and Ebling (2005) believed to better understand adolescents, one must first understand how they construe their experiences that include the full range of their mental processes and interpretations.

Developmental theorists like Rogers (1989) believed the process of becoming fully functioning is supported and encouraged throughout life by people who are important to us, the significant others such as parents. This is helpful when parents provide adolescents with unconditional positive regard through which they perceive that they are loved, respected, and able to share their views. For example, when adolescents voice their opinions or concerns about something, parents can demonstrate unconditional positive regard by acknowledging and respecting their voice rather than simply reciprocating with resentment and hostility (Carig & Baucum, 2002). Rogers (1989) also stressed the importance of agreement between how people see themselves and how they hope to be seen by others. In other words, a parent may intend the message conveyed to be positive, supportive, and constructive. According to Landry et al. (2006), despite their intentions, the adolescent may perceive the message as negative, unhelpful, and unsupportive. Listening to what adolescents have to say about their interpretation and perception of a message can shed light on ways to enhance the parent-adolescent relationship.

Rogers (1989) emphasized that behavior is guided by each person's unique actualizing tendency and that all behavior has a need for positive regard. The actualizing tendency moves people toward increased autonomy and self-sufficiency, thereby, expanding their experiences and fostering personal growth. In essence, the actualizing tendency guides people towards positive, constructive, and adaptive behavior rather than toward destructive or maladaptive behavior (Craig & Baucum, 2002). Positive regard is positive social feedback taking the form of acceptance, respect, warmth, and love (Rogers). Positive regard is essential for the healthy development in children (Rogers). Jones and Meredith (1996) contended that for infants and children, positive regard comes exclusively from external sources; parents, older children, and other adults. As children develop more autonomy and a sense of self, they are able to provide their own internal positive regard. All children deserve supportive environments that nurture their development and promote opportunities.

Bronfenbrenner (1995) believed that the meanings adolescents attach to opportunities (granted or withheld) and other experiences with their parents affect developmental outcome. Therefore, one of the most important jobs for parents is to provide support and opportunities in a constructive manner rather than to try and shape adolescents (Scarr, 1996). In this way, the adolescent's ability to move beyond a parent specific position to one of his or her own will increase autonomy. This study differs from prior research by examining communication with parents from adolescents' point of view. To do this, the PACS developed by Barnes and Olson (1982) will be used to assess open and problematic communication between adolescents and their parents. The PACS scale is explained in detail in chapter 3.

Adolescents as Sources of Information

Adolescents can be valuable sources of information for parents (Garth & Aroni, 2003; Nichols, 2005; Yamamato, 1993). According to Garbarino and Scott (1992), when adolescents are talking, they are not just repeating words and sentences that they have heard others say. Rather, when they talk, they provide rich opportunities to hear their minds at work actively trying to make sense of the world around them. According to multiple researchers (Brannen, 2002; Garbarino & Scott, 1992; Harter, 1990; Nichols, 2005), their ideas and views reflect the inferences and connections that they have been able to make based on their knowledge, observations, and experiences in life.

Understanding all children's emotional responses from their point of view plays an important role in good parenting and autonomy development (Levine et al., 1999). For example, 75 parents and children, ages 3 to 6 years old, participated in a study to recall events that evoked happiness, sadness, anger, and fear in their children (Levine et al.). Parents and children participated individually in interviews in which they were asked to recall four emotional events. Facial, verbal, and behavioral expressions of emotions were considered as factors to explain how they felt with younger children. Results indicated that agreement between parent and children concerning how the child felt varied as a function of emotion (Levine et al.). Therefore, parent-child relationships benefit greatly when parents try to understand how events have affected the emotions, needs, and desires of the children. If parents try to understand and recount events from their children's perspective, they are more likely to establish cooperative and harmonious relationship. On the other hand, disagreements about emotions between parents and children could be accounted for by parents' failure to identify their children's goals (Levine et al.) To illustrate, Levine et al reported on a mother's report of how happy her son was when she took him grocery shopping: They reported:

> According to the mother, her son enjoyed the trip because it fulfilled his goal of having his mother to himself. When the child was asked about the shopping trip, he remembered it clearly but said it made him feel sad. He was sad because he knew that when he went shopping with his mother, his older brothers would go in his room, play with his favorite toys, and eat his candy Gummy Worms. (p. 801)

Thus, for the child, going on a shopping trip with his mother represented the failure of set goals of which his mother was unaware or at least did not acknowledge (Levine et al. They believed that it is important for parents to validate, rather than deny the emotions that their children experience and report.

During adolescence, parents can provide their adolescents with opportunities for social, emotional, and intellectual development that contribute to autonomy. For adolescents, parents are the primary source of support in the process of problem-solving and social experiences (Eisenberg et al., 2001; Landry et al., 2006). Mothers and fathers do this in many ways both directly and indirectly. For instance, a parent can make an activity more interesting for the adolescent by getting involved and managing the demands of the task (Santrock, 1999). Parents can also make the activity more autonomously challenging by encouraging the adolescent to discover ways to complete the task through their own initiative and creativity (Santrock). Parents can further encourage the adolescent to self disclose their feelings and thoughts, or they can discourage the adolescent from expressing their opinions and views (Soenens et al., 2006). For example, a study examined relations between parenting dimensions and self disclosure, perceived parental knowledge, and problem behaviors (Soenens et al). The sample population included 348 boys and girls from three schools with a mean age of 17 years old, 10th to 12th graders. A questionnaire was used in the study with the parents and adolescents answering five items tapping adolescents' voluntary self-disclosure. Results of the study showed that high responsiveness, high behavioral control, and low psychological control are independent predictors of self-disclosure (Soenens et al). Self-disclosure was positively associated with perceived parental knowledge. Parenting not only affected parental knowledge and problem behavior through adolescents' self-disclosure but also showed a direct path to perceived parental knowledge. Results of this study suggest that, through parenting, parents might create a family climate that fosters the disclosure of personal information by their children (Soenens et al). The adolescent's observation and perception of parental behaviors and responsiveness during these interactions may be viewed by the adolescent as providing support for their cognitive skills and autonomous development (Anan & Barnett, 1999; Parke & Buriel, 1997) or authoritative and threatening (Braine et al., 1997), thereby, diminishing opportunities to develop autonomy (Harter, 1998).

Another study by Grolnick et al (1997) was conducted to examine children and adolescents' perception of their parents, their motivation, and their performance in school. Participants included 456 children in grades 3 through 6 from 20 classrooms in a large town. The school district was a mix of farm families and families in which parents commuted to work in a nearby city. The sample was largely White and heterogeneous in SES. The Children Perception of Parent Scale was used to measure perception of control understanding, perceived competence, and perceived autonomy. The parents were given a self-report to complete for the study. Motivation was hypothesized to mediate between children and adolescents' perception of their parents and school performance. Results showed that perceived maternal autonomy support, understanding, and involvement were positively associated with competence and autonomy. With fathers, only perceived autonomy support was related to competence and autonomy. Thus, children and adolescents' perceptions of the parents may stem in part from differences between mothers and fathers in their expectations for children's behavior (Grolnick et al., 1997). The POPS developed by Grolnick, Deci, and Ryan (1991, will be used in this study to assess adolescents' perception of the degree to which their parents are autonomy supportive and the degree to which their parents are controlling. This study differs from others in that adolescents' perceptions will be measured from four different ethnic groups. The POPS will be described in detail in chapter 3.

In recent years adolescents have been asked to give their views on certain familial experiences in their lives. Yet, there are reservations in some people's minds as to whether or not adolescents know themselves well enough to be able to give dependable responses to questions about themselves (Levine et al., 2006). They argued that expert opinions have typically been used to judge the severity of the given experience for adolescents, largely due to uncertainty on the part of adults. Yamamato (1993) believed that what grownups see and judge from the outside might not be the same as what adolescents feel and think on the inside. Studies with adolescents as young as elementary school ages show their judgments are both discriminating and stable over time (Yamamoto). For example, different groups of 197 U.S. professionals (clinicians, school psychologists, teachers, nurses, social workers, and speech pathologists) and 197 children were asked to respond to the same 20 life events. Children were asked to rate how upsetting each event was to them individually. The adult professionals participating were asked to report on how upsetting they thought the event would be for the children. Examples of the life events were losing a parent, going blind, academic retention, wetting in class, getting lost, sent to principal, and going to the dentist. Results showed close agreement was evident among children differing in age, sex, ethnicity, and social class, on the overall assessment of how various life events affect them. Overall, the findings did not give much support to the idea that, "adult's view of the children would correspond closely with the young's own perspectives" (p. 22). Results of the study showed that, "children do not the initially respond to many events the same as adults do" (p. 22). In other words, children may perceive, interpret, and respond to the same situation in a different way than their parents. It is the child's own view that serves as a guide to feel, act, and think in a certain way. Yamamoto reported:

Grownups rush into the world of little people fully intending to correct in their lives, what they see as defects. Grownups become so absorbed and serious about what they regard to be the only way to serve the welfare of the children that they cease to entertain any other possibilities and fail to see inherent potential in the children themselves. (p. 145)

Dweck and Kaminis (1999) suggested that "if parents wish to tune in to children's inside-out views they must allow the child to show them by watching them, listening to them, and remaining receptive to their experiences" (p. 23). Likewise, Nichols (2005) believed that parents should be free of blame and guilt and become genuinely interested in children and adolescents' feelings and experiences.

Dweck and Kaminis (1999) asserted that adolescents are not passively programmed, although they frequently develop patterns of behaviors in reaction to what they see their parents doing. The role of parents in relation to each adolescent is important because children all ages always see their parents as essential to their survival (Santrock, 1999). Satir (1988) suggested that supportive parents should engage in congruent communication with their children. For example, a study examined associations among family discord, caregiver communication quality about emotionally stressful events, and children's' internal representations of family security in 50 preschool children and their primary caregivers (Winters et al., 2006). Findings indicated that children exhibiting the highest level of secure representation of the family experienced a consistency between low levels of family discord and communications emphasizing family security. Incongruence between family experiences and communication reflected in high levels of family discord and communications underscoring family security was associated with the lowest level of child secure representations. Results suggested that child representations hinge on the fit between caregiver communication quality and family security (Winters et al.). Children and adolescents' interpretation of family events may hinge on the interaction between exposure to family stress and parental discussion aimed at buffering them and thereby, restricting their understanding of events (Winters et al.). If parents effectively communicate with children and adolescents in ways that lessen their concerns in the face of stressful family circumstances, then communication would serve as a protective factor in the relationship (Winters et al., 2006). They argued that if parents buffer children and adolescents from communicating their interpretations of family events, autonomy diminishes and children may experience stress themselves. Parents are to listen, acknowledge, appreciate, and allow the children and adolescents to complain (Nichols, 2005), and give them information needed to develop autonomy both within and outside the family. Nichols asserted that parents need to provide greater mutuality and more opportunities for all children to voice their concerns and share their views, thereby, promoting autonomy development. Similarly, Yamamato (1993) believed adolescents become more autonomous and better able to react to life circumstances when they react to external demands on their own accord.

Even though some theorists such as Bandura (1986; 2001) and Bronfenbrenner (1995) have suggested that adolescents' phenomenal view of their socializing environment is of considerable importance, research on the adolescent's perspective remains unexplored. This study extended previous work by exploring whether there was a relationship between adolescents' beliefs about parental support to express their views and autonomy development. To do this, the RAI of the SRQ-A will be used to measure autonomy and the PACS, developed by Barnes and Olson (1982) will be used to assess open and problematic communication with both parents. The SRQ-A and PACS are explained in detail in chapter 3.

Decision Input

According to multiple researchers (Eccles et al., 1996; Hallestrom, 2004; Nichols, 2005), an important component of family relations during adolescence is the opportunity for adolescents to have increased input into decisions about issues that affect their daily lives. Parental encouragement of adolescents to participate in decision-making promotes appropriate levels of individuality and autonomy by demonstrating to adolescents that their points of view are important (Buddin, 1999). The UN Convention on the Rights of the Child formulated the needs of all children to have input into decisions as a human right (Article 3, 1989). According to Hallestrom, even though autonomy, integrity, and competence are at times, difficult to relate to practice, ethical duties of health professionals include the obligation to enhance their patients' competence and promote the ability to participate. For example, a study was conducted to observe 24 children and 35 parents during the adolescent's hospitalization and situations including a decision-making process (Hallestrom). Analysis included assessing and grading both adolescent's and parent's involvement in decisions according to a five-level scale of different degrees of respect. Results showed that both adolescents and parents had varying abilities to become involved in the decision-making process. The study suggested that promoting children's rights is an important role for professionals. Hallstrom suggested that having a voice in decision-making helps the child develop a sense of him-herself as a person and gives the parents a feeling that they are part of a team promoting optimal care for their children.

Another study was conducted investigating parental autonomy granting, adolescent's decision making input, and parental knowledge of adolescent's daily experiences (Bumpus et al., 2001). Home interviews and adolescent questionnaires were administered to 194 families with children between ages 12 and 15 years old. Parents and adolescents considered eight domains; chores, appearance, homework and schoolwork, social life, bedtime and curfew, health, participation in activities, and money. Respondents selected one of the following for each domain; youth alone, mother, father, either parents, nobody. Results revealed that in families where mothers held more traditional attitudes, adolescents experienced fewer decision-making opportunities than from less traditional families. Mother and fathers perceptions of decision making differed. In addition, firstborns were granted more autonomy opportunities. Boys were granted more autonomy opportunities than girls. Parents with more traditional attitudes towards gender role did not grant their sons with high levels of autonomy. Adolescent's report of their decision-making was uncorrelated with parents (Bumpus et al.). Garbarino (1995) suggested that adolescents spontaneously organize their perceptions, thoughts, and beliefs about events, other people, and situations in simple meaningful ways that makes sense to them. Even though their perceptions and points of view about autonomy may differ from parent (Garbarino), they do hold beliefs and right to opinions (Melton, 1996). According to Garbarino and Scott (1992), no matter how chaotic or arbitrary it may seem to others, adolescents' interpretation of events and people is important. Granting opportunities for adolescents to express their views and opinions is equally important.

Voice and Adolescents' Rights

According to Stepp (2000), given the opportunity, adolescents can teach parents and other adults something about raising them. Yet, because adult reactions focus on issues remote to adolescents, they frequently make errors in misjudging the significance of children's invested feelings and their rights to opinions (Krebs & Denton; 2005; Yamamato, 1993). For example, a study conducted on student retention in the classroom involved 1000 parents, 200 school teachers, 40 principals, and 26,000 students in a large school district (Yamamoto). The overall retention rate from kindergarten through 12th grade was 10%. Parents, teachers, and principles were required to give their views about who should have the final say on whether or not a child should be retained for another year. Results showed that 40% of parents said the teacher and 20% said the parent. In contrast, 66% of teachers named the teacher followed by 13% who said the teacher and principal. Regarding the principals, 54% of them said the principal and 23% named the teacher. Findings revealed that virtually everyone ignored the adolescent in considering the retention decision. Not any of the teachers or principals even remotely entertained the idea that perhaps the adolescent in question should be the one who makes the final judgment. Even among parents, only 4 out of 1000 said they would give voice to the adolescent as the ultimate decision maker (Yamamoto). Every person has the right to input and make decisions on the matters most directly affecting him or her. The adolescents who were directly affected by the experience of the retention should have had a voice in this decision (Yamamato, 1993). He further explained:

> While youngsters continue quite visibly to grow, there is also room for grown-ups to grow by becoming more clearly aware of their own basic attitudes and routine practices as regards to the young ones. Big people frequently make errors in misjudging the significance of little people's creations and invested feelings. Obviously, what a person has carved out of his or her life, whether it is in words or in play, carries a special meaning to that person. How swiftly we grownups forget. Even before fully acknowledging that uniqueness, that novelty, adults rush in with comparative judgments on the skill, taste, and merit of the young. It is not that children will not take fair, honest, and constructive criticism, but that such comments are usually premature and off target. (p.127)

According to the UN Convention on the Rights of the Child (UN General Assembly, 1989), respect for the dignity of all children is compatible with provision of those elements important to their growth as full members of the community (Hart, 1991a; 1991b; Melton, 1996; 2005a; 2005b). Children are "indeed persons and concerns with special rights for all children should not be used to negate or ignore that they are shared by all humanity" (p.1235). Kochanska (2002) argued that from a very early age, freedom is meaningful and reinforcing, and its availability increases children and adolescents' investment in education, treatment, and their sense of personal control.

Whether physical as in corporeal punishment or psychological as in accusations of lying, adolescents also experience assaults on their personal integrity (Hart, 1991b). Thorkildsen, Sodonis, and White-McNulty (2004) assumed that some aspects of adolescents' knowledge would be resistant to new information and that perceptions would be distorted. They believed that when acquiring new knowledge, most adolescents develop the ability to think abstractly and learn to reason about fairness. For example, in a study with 128 adolescents from grades 9 though 12 were interviewed about the effectiveness and fairness of practices for teaching controversial and non controversial science topics in school. Each participant was interviewed about 20 minutes. Results showed that adolescent's beliefs about the practice of lecturing differed considerably for two science topics. McNemar tests indicated that most adolescents found lectures effective, autonomy supportive, and fair when used with non-controversial topics than when used to teach controversial topics. Results from adolescent's decisions and justifications also verified their ability to consider the welfare of all learners (Thorkildsen et al.). Respect for the dignity of all children is not only an ethical obligation, but it is also sound public policy. Taking all children seriously is likely to result in improved child welfare (Thorkildsen et al.), socialization (Hart, 1991a; Tenenbaum & Leaper, 2003) and autonomy (Melton, 2005a). Only when children and adolescents are "taken seriously will they feel a part of the community" (Melton 2005b, p. 923). Only then will they be "empowered to act as autonomous beings in support of the commonwealth" (p. 923). Only then will they have the "opportunity to develop the skills and values that will enable them to function ultimately as productive citizens who care about, both, their home, community, and global community" (Hart, 1991b, p. 58).

During adolescence, the willingness to take adolescents seriously is even more important when it comes to their feelings and emotions (Yamamato, 1993). Even when they do not recognize those feelings and cannot express them in words, what adolescents feel in their hearts and sense in the whole body is as significant if not more so, than what they think and say (Yamamoto). He believed, "everyone young and old constructs his or her own reality, and that reality, no matter how ludicrous or incoherent it might appear to others, makes sense to that particular person" (p. 21). Adolescence can be regarded as "a new discovery of gradually redefining civilization" (p.21). This view makes adolescents into a "special class, not to control or mold them, rather, to conserve them into a natural wonder" (Adams et al., 1971, p. 3-4). Unless grownups are willing to listen and remain receptive to adolescents' views, they will not learn from them or understand the adolescent's world (Yamamoto). On one hand, parents are able to provide protection, opportunities, and conditions conducive to autonomy development. On the other hand, "lest we are careful, we will mold the very children who will take our place when we die into the same thing which destroyed the world in the first-place; hate, wars, bigotry, sex, rape, and crime" (p. 23). The purpose of study is to examine adolescents' beliefs about whether they have parental support to express their views and thereby, developing greater autonomy.

Ethnicity, Communication, and Values

As soon as adolescents begin to have conversations with others and are able to have insight into their social communications, they already have access to their cultural values and beliefs (Ahmed, 2002). According to multiple researchers (Damon, 1990; Davalos et al., 2005; Stevenson-Hinde, 1998), both culture and values are factors that shape adolescents' social experience in ways that influence their reasoning, beliefs, and ways of communicating. They suggested that culture makes a difference because there is wide discrepancy in values communicated to adolescents by their parents in societies across the world.

Despite variations among cultures on how The U. N. Convention on Rights of the Child (U.N. General Assembly, 1989) is understood and interpreted, it is designed to be a worldwide, comprehensive guide to defining and implementing all children's rights (Murphy-Berman, Levesque, & Weisz, 1996). For example, among cultures, "it may be difficult for some individuals to imagine children as having rights apart from their parents" (Murphy-Berman et al., 1996, p. 1258). Yet, the U.N. Convention on the Rights of the Child was drafted over a 10 year period of time by a diversity of international views (Melton, 1991a; 1991b; 1996; Murphy-Berman et al.). Major contributors to the drafting of the Convention included representatives from the United States, France, the Netherlands, Norway, the United Kingdom, Sweden, Denmark, Germany, Italy, Russia (formerly the U.S.S.R.), and Poland. Despite this variety of international input, certain cultural viewpoints may have been more represented than others. For instance, only Latin American countries, 2 Asian countries, and 3 of 51 African states participated in all nine drafting sessions of the Convention. "Some of the countries that were most heavily involved in the drafting meetings such as the United States were among those most reluctant to ratify it" (Murphy-Berman et al., p. 1257). Therefore, within cultures, "the question becomes how to balance needs for autonomy and ways to enhance rather than compete with existing cultural values" (p. 1257). Davalos et al. (2005) and Kowal, Kramer, Krull, and Crick (2002), suggested that because values are mediated through social communication, cultural discrepancies will lead to variations in the way adolescents perceive and interpret this information. Nonetheless, that balance should include "autonomous participation and self-expression" (Murphy-Berman et al., p. 1260).

To illustrate the effect of culture on communication, a study was conducted to examine the role of perceived parental school support and family communication in the context of delinquent behaviors in Mexican and White non Latino adolescents (Davalos et al., 2005). Family communication was defined as "the degree to which adolescents endorsed that communication with their parents about a variety of topics" (p. 57). Participants included 576 school dropouts (7th to 12th graders) and youths still enrolled in school. Surveys were administered to three school districts in the southwestern region of the United States from an urban population of 40,000 and a small community of 30,000. The Parental School Support scale was used to assess adolescent's perceptions of parental support for academic goals. The Family Communication Scale was used to measure the level and depth of communication in the family as reported by the adolescents. Results demonstrated that adolescents' perceptions of family communication and parental school support were related to the likelihood of committing delinquent acts as well as experience distress that affects school performance. Findings also suggested that delinquency is related to perceived lack of communication in families, that is, the greater the endorsement of family communication, the less likely the individual is to engage in all types of delinquent behavior. There were no significant differences in gender or ethnicity in perceived levels of family communication and parental support. "Those adolescents who feel that their families are not invested in their lives may conclude that, if their parents do not care about our lives, who else possibly could?" (p.65). This study will extend to other studies in that it examines adolescents in four different ethnic groups beliefs about whether they have parental support to express their views.

According to Camras, Chen, Bakeman, Norris, and Cain (2006, the style of communicating itself is culturally related. They suggested that social scientists from a variety of disciplines have concurred that emotional expressions differ greatly across cultures. For example, research was conducted documenting differences in Chinese and European American children's facial expressivity (Camras et al.). Participants were adopted and non adopted 3 years olds (45 European girls and 42 Chinese girls) divided into four groups. They responded to emotionally evocative slides and an odor stimulus. Results showed that European American girls smiled more than Mainland Chinese and Chinese American girls scored higher for disgust-related expressions and overall expressivity. Adopted Chinese girls showed more disgust-related expressions than Mainland Chinese girls. Results suggest that culture and family environment influences facial expressions, creating differences among children of the same ethnicity (Camaras et al.). They suggested that verbal and nonverbal communication, such as eye movement, posture, and facial expressions convey meaning interpreted within the culture framework of the child and parent.

Similarly, the meanings of silence in one ethnic group may be considered good manners. Yet, according to researchers Choo (2002) and Pingerhughes et al. (2000), silence in another group may be considered a form of rudeness, an expression of fear, or sign of low intelligence. Subsequently, the original intent of silence itself can be misinterpreted. Stepp (2000) believed that for many children and adolescents, moments and stretches of silence can be the means for important statements. "When the child falls silent, we should keep our eyes open and pay attention to the wordless narration that can take place as the child uses his or her face, arms or legs to convey a message" (p. 66). She believed, "if adults have their own way of silently making statements, why can't children?" (p. 66). Likewise, Shafer and Gordon (1995) suggested giving children and adolescents' "permission to be silent and don't be too quick to react" (p.117). They believed that adults should listen and make an effort "to read between the lines to discover whether a problem exists" (p.117). Listening and observing are opportunities to learn how to "see the world from the child's viewpoint and what the child's life issues are" (p.117).

Family systems theory posited that increased understanding of adolescents' expression and forms of communication is a harmonious form of family relatedness. Theorists Bronfenbrenner (1995) and Minuchin (1985) believed that families consist of interdependent members whose functioning cannot be understood in isolation of one another. Whereas parents may have biases when acknowledging the adolescents' beliefs and ways of thinking, listening to what adolescents have to say and attempting to understand their expressions will help to avoid misinterpretations.

This further enhances family relatedness and adolescents' autonomous development. Adolescents' and children's voice continues to be ignored and unexplored. For example, a study was conducted interviewing White parents and immigrant Chinese parents of children between the ages of 3 and 7 years old (Rothbaum et al., 2000a). Each culture was represented by 20 mothers and 20 fathers from different families with equal number of boys and girls (Rothbaum et al.). They were all intact families, predominantly upper middle class and highly educated. In consideration of children voices, the theme was whose point of view or voice is salient when parents make decisions about their care. The code "child voice" was used when parents took into account the child's desires and preferences. The code "voice over" was used when parents indicated that they knew what was best for the child without relying on the child's desires or preferences (p. 339). Results showed that White parents were more likely than immigrant-Chinese parents to consider their children desires and preferences (child voice) when making decisions about their children's need for care and physical closeness and less likely to presume knowledge of their children's needs (voice over), but only for privacy activities. Most of Chinese (60%) evidenced only voice over (as compared with only 25% of Whites), whereas most Whites (63%) evidenced both child voice and voice over as compared with only 28% of immigrant Chinese. Results of the study also suggest that children's voices about physical closeness and family relatedness are thought about differently among immigrant Chinese and Whites parents (Rothbaum et al).

Until recently it has been assumed that children younger than 8 years old could not provide "psychometrically sound self-reports" (Harter, 1998, p. 895). According to Measelle, John, Ablow, Cowan, and Cowan (2005), as children turn 4 years old and move into early and then middle childhood, there is a marked shift in their capacity to process and organize complex information in a coherent and useful manner. For example, 110 families with children, ages 5 through 7 were participants in a longitudinal study of transition to school (Measelle et al.). Families were recruited from preschools, daycares, and the local media. Of the families, 21% were Black, Hispanic, or Asian American ethnicity. The remaining 79% were White. Self-reports of the Big Five personality traits were measured with the Berkeley Puppet Interview (BPI) were used to interview children. Results showed that children as young as 5 years of age were able to describe themselves fairly consistently on the Big Five dimensions on the basis of their responses to the BPI. At very least, by ages 6 to 7, young children's self perception on the Big Five demonstrated the level of distinctiveness seen for the same item set in college-age adults (Measelle et al.). Although not quite as internally consistent as the self reports provided by comparison of college students, the differences were generally small. By age 6, children's self-reports on Agreeableness, Conscientiousness, and Neuroticism were as consistent as those of college students (Measelle et al.). Therefore, considering children's growing capacities to report reliably and validly on their personality, "they may well be the best informants about their internal states" (p. 471). Research is needed examining children views as compared with their parents. This study will build on previous research by exploring if differences exist among ethnic groups in children's beliefs of parental support to express their views and autonomy development.

Bandura (2001) suggested that as children move from childhood to adolescence, they begin to face critical challenges to developing a coherent, consolidated sense of self that affects autonomy. The true self is described as the "real me inside and what I really think and feel," (Harter et al., 1998, p. 892) whereas the "false self includes being phony and putting on an act" (p. 892). One vehicle through which "true self-behaviors" (p. 892) are typically communicated by adolescents is verbally such as "expressing their true opinions and telling people what they really feel or believe inside" (Harter, 1998, p. 289). In contrast, "false self behaviors are described as not saying what you think, expressing things you don't really believe or feel, not stating your true opinion, and saying what you think people want to hear" (p. 289). For example, in a study with 25 males and 25 females, authors examined level of self-reported voice with parents, teachers, male classmates, female classmates, and close friends between both male and female high school students. Findings revealed no gender differences or evidence that voice declines in female adolescents. For both genders, perceived support for voice was predictive of level of voice. Feminine girls reported lower levels of voice than did androgynous girls in public (but not private) relational contexts. Lower levels of voice were associated with more negative evaluations of self worth (Harter et al., 1998). Consistent with Gilligan's (1993) findings, "loss of voice" (p. 290) is referred to namely as, "suppression of one's thoughts and opinions" (p. 290), and thereby, diminishing autonomy.

To further explore examples when true feelings are not expressed a study was conducted by Chapman et al (2004) with over 1,000 adolescents to obtain views about living in foster care. Adolescents reported high satisfaction with living arrangement and their caregivers. Additionally, adolescents living in traditional foster care were more satisfied than those in group placements. Most of the adolescents reported beliefs that their foster parents were trying to help them and many reported a variety of positive changes in their life as a result of the placements. Although finding showed that adolescents' views of out-of-home placement are uniformly positive, other factors may have influenced their responses; contact with biological family, comfort with out of home care, and experiences in local schools and neighborhoods. However, limitations of the study suggest first, the adolescents' answers about their caregivers may reflect social desirability rather than true feelings (Chapman et al.). They also suggested that adolescents may not have felt comfortable enough in the interview setting to share more negative views about their current placements and may not have understood, despite explanations that interviewers had no decision-making power over their future. In any event, multiple researchers (Buddin, 1999; Harter et al., 1998; Stepp, 2000), suggested that regardless of the setting, adolescents need supportive opportunities to voice their opinions and views about factors that impact on their development.

Autonomy and Individuation

Adolescents and having their parents' support to communicate with them is an important aspect of autonomy development. Autonomous support is a feature of parental behavior that includes responsiveness (Bufe, 1997), reflecting (Buddin, 1999), and validating the adolescents' opinions, feelings, and perspectives (Harter et al., 1998). Culture also plays a large part in this process. According to Erikson (1986), each adolescent's ability to deal with the most significant tasks or crisis of psychosocial development also involves their parents. He pointed out that it would be a mistake to assume that autonomy develops and a sense of identity is achieved primarily through the adolescents' complete surrender and adaptation to social roles and norms. Erikson's second stage of development, autonomy versus shame and doubt begins as early as age one to three. After gaining trust in their parents, the child's task is to develop a healthy independence that continues throughout childhood to adolescence. Yet, during childhood, if children are restrained too much or punished too harshly, they are likely to develop a sense of shame and doubt (Erikson). Likewise, Piaget's (1965; 1966) theory, suggested that autonomous morality is the second stage of moral development and is displayed by adolescents 10 years of age and older. When interpreting an act, adolescents are able to consider the intentions of the act. As adolescents seek autonomy and responsibility, parents may have an urge to take stronger control over them (Chirkov et al., 2003; Stevenson-Hinde, 1998). The ability to support autonomy while gaining control over their behaviors is acquired through appropriate parent's reactions to the adolescent's desire (Levine et al., 1999). Consideration should be given to their limited knowledge to make appropriate or mature decisions in all areas of life. Piaget (1966) believed that "we ourselves adopt the point of view, not of the adult conscience but of the child's morality" (p. 2). As adolescents seek to develop autonomy, rather than taking control in those areas where adolescents can make reasonable decisions for themselves, parents can continue to provide guidance and support (Chirkov et al.; Levesque et al., 2004; Stevenson-Hinde). If adolescents perceive parental behaviors as supportive and encouraging, autonomy develops.

According to the SDT, support for individuation, autonomy, and competence are essential for growth and well being in any learning environment (Ryan & Deci, 2000). A study examined the role of autonomy and competence in 2 German and 2 U.S. university settings (Levesque et al., 2004). Results showed that German students felt significantly more autonomous and less competent that U.S. students. Perceived pressures and positive informational feedback were modeled as antecedents of autonomy and competence, whereas well-being was examined as a consequence. Autonomous teachers were found to enhance autonomous motivation and the desire for challenge in their students. In addition, autonomy-supportive parents had more autonomous college level children, who in turn better adjusted in school (Levesque et al.). They argued that the importance of an autonomy-supportive social context to enhance feelings of autonomy and individuation has been supported at all levels of schooling from elementary education to college to postgraduate education.

According to Ryan and Deci (2000), the SDT maintained that autonomous motivation is universally important and should predict better learning and high well being even among Chinese students. A five point Likert scale and the SRQ-A developed by Ryan and Connell (1989) were used in a study with 153 Chinese participants. Ninety-three were female and 57 were male (Vansteenkiste et al., 2004). Three participants did not provide their gender. Findings from both studies indicated that autonomous study motivation positively predicts adaptive learning attitudes, academic success, and personal well-being, whereas controlled motivation was associated with high drop-out rates, maladaptive learning attitudes, and ill-being (Vansteenkiste et al.). In addition, autonomy-supportive parents find it important that their adolescents no longer rely on them for advice and support but are able to stand on their own feet, act independently of their parents, and attain individuality (Vansteenkiste et al.). According to the SDT, autonomy is not defined in terms of independence. Rather, autonomy is a psychological need and its satisfaction is critical for all individual's optimal development Chirkov et al., 2003). Autonomy is emphasized depending on the cultural context and reflects the "self-endorsement of actions on an inner, intra-individual level" (p. 98).

Adolescents occupy a unique place in every ethnic group and expectations for them are enormously varied. Among groups, therefore, adolescents' beliefs are likely to vary as well. Factors that influence adolescents' beliefs reflect indigenous family values and goals that differ from one society to the next (Rothbaum et al., 2000b). For example, beginning in infancy, Japanese parents prefer to anticipate their children's needs by relying on situational cues. At times, this means identifying situations that may be stressful for their infants and taking steps to minimize the stress. On the other hand, parents in the United States prefer to wait for their children to communicate their needs before taking steps to meet those needs. The difference between expressions of sensitivity and responsiveness suggests that parenting in Japanese families has more to do with the emotional closeness and helping infants regulate their emotional states Rothbaum et al.) They suggested that for parents in the United States, responsiveness has more to do with encouragement and whenever possible, respecting children's autonomous efforts to satisfy those needs..

A study was conducted to examine the process whereby attachment and other social and cognitive factors contribute to social and emotional adjustment, leading to autonomy (Anan & Barnett, 1999). Participants were 69 African American children recruited from several Head Start type preschool programs with 4 years old in 56 families. Attachment and sociability were assessed using the Strange Situation. Results showed that attachment predicted perceived social support. Insecure attachment predicted self-reports of behavior problems and parental support of internalizing problems. Perceived support was associated with positively and significantly viewing ambiguously depicted actions as prosocial rather than aggressive. Perceived social support was found to mediate the relation between attachment and adjustment. Results suggested that behaviorally mediated strategies for relating to caregivers in early childhood predict generalized social perception, thought, and emotion at later ages (Anan & Barnett).

Additional studies by Chen et al (2000) and Rothbaum et al (2000b) suggested that parental behaviors among Japanese involve sensitivity to encourage children's dependence on their mothers. In contrast, United States parents encourage infant exploration of their environment. In Japan, mothers also direct the child's attention to social objects, particularly; themselves rather than to physical objects like United States parents (Chen et al.). Japanese sensitivity is seen as responsive to infants needs for social engagement (Chen et al.). In the United States, sensitivity is seen as responsive to the children's need for individuation leading to autonomy development (Rothbaum et al). Although parental warmth and control are classical dimensions in the parenting literature, children of indulgent parents are likely to be "spoiled" (Rothbaum et al., p.1096) and develop "self centeredness and negative attitudes" (p. 1096). Indulgent parents are often "highly protective and discourage exploratory behaviors in children" (Chen et al., p. 404). As a result, their children may have few opportunities to develop autonomy and individuation during adolescence. Again, no studies on adolescents' views of how they develop autonomy have been conducted.

Another study was conducted examining parental warmth, control, and indulgence on children's social, academic, and psychological adjustment (Chen et al., 2000). The sample included self reports from 258 sixth grades boys (137) and girls (121) in two schools in the People's Republic of China. Adolescents' reports of parenting styles were assessed using the Children's Report of Parent Behavior Inventory (CRPBI) developed by Schafer (1965). It was found that paternal indulgence had significant and negative contributions to the prediction of later leadership, social competence, and academic achievement, as well as being related positively to later aggressive, disruptive behaviors. Maternal warmth had significant contributions to the predictions of emotional adjustment, social, and school achievement. Therefore, fathers and mothers may be equally involved in childrearing in Chinese families (Chen et al., 2000). Even though adolescents are more likely to turn to mothers for emotional support, physical needs, and help in dealing with problems in daily life (Lee, Choe, & Ngo, 2000), it is important for both parents to encourage and provide opportunities for autonomy.

Emotional openness is another factor associated with individuation and autonomy in children all ages (Levine et al., 1999). According to Soto et al. (2005), ethnographic accounts suggested that emotions are moderated in Chinese cultures and expressed openly in Mexican cultures. The authors tested this notion by comparing subjective, behavioral, and physiological aspects of emotional responses to 3 (warned, unwarned, instructed to inhibit responding) aversive acoustic startle stimuli in 95 Chinese American and 64 Mexican Americans between ages 18 and 30 months. Subjective reports were consistent with ethnographic accounts; Chinese Americans reported experiencing significantly less emotion than Mexican Americans across all three startle conditions. Few cultural differences were found in emotional behavior or physiology, suggesting that these aspects of emotions are less susceptible to cultural influence (Soto et al.). They believe that "emotions are the cornerstone of our social world affecting our interactions with others in countless ways" (p. 154).

Attachment theorists believe emotional openness is important to all children's well-being (Ainsworth, 1989; Bowlby, 1989). According to Fosco and Grych (2007), nothing helps a child more than being able to express feelings candidly, directly, and spontaneously. In support, Florsheim, Tolan, and Gorman-Smith (1996) contended that children's feelings of security are associated with their sensitive, open communication with parents, particularly in the United States. Emotional openness may less likely to be seen as a desirable quality in Japan where children are encouraged to keep hostile feelings to themselves. Japanese parents tend to discourage these behaviors to preserve social harmony. If hostile feelings are expressed it probably means the relationship is beyond repair (Florsheim et al., 1996). Latino families tend to be more cohesive and warmer than European American and African American families suggesting that emotional climate does vary across ethnic groups (Florsheim et al., 1996). For example, a study was conducted to test the hypotheses that open communication encourages adolescents to practice the values and norms embedded in the parents' messages. The study examined whether parental communication with children about drugs and sex will deter involvement in risk behavior (Wills, Gibbons, Gerrard, Murray, & Brody, 2003). The study included 297 Black adolescents, ages 10 to 14, and their parents from three different states. Parents and adolescents were interviewed separately. The PACS was used in this study. Results showed that parent adolescent communication had a path to unfavorable prototypes of substance users; quality of parent adolescent relationship had paths to good self-control, higher resistance efficacy, and unfavorable prototypes of sexually active teens. Results gave some support for parent-child communication as a unique protective construct in regards to openness (Wills et al.). In contrast, a study with 165 mother-adolescent dyads of European or Latino descent was conducted to see if patterns about conflicts, sexuality, and Acquired Immune Deficiency Syndrome (AIDS) vary by culture, age, and situation (Lefkowitz, Romo, Corona, Au, & Sigman, 2000). Results showed that Latino American mothers dominated conversations more then European American mothers, independent of socioeconomic status. Mothers dominated conversations about sexuality and AIDS more than conversations about conflicts. Mothers of older adolescents reacted more negatively and older adolescents reported less satisfaction, less openness, and more sexual discussions with persons other than their mothers. Latino American mothers who dominated conversations more reported more openness and satisfaction. When mothers dominated conversations more, adolescents had lower AIDS knowledge (Lefkowitz et al). Therefore, the way mother and children communicate has important implications for children's development.

The self-determination theory argued that people from all cultures share basic psychological needs for autonomy, competence, and relatedness (Ryan & Deci, 2000). They contended the primary controversy has concerned the need for autonomy. A study was conducted on the self-determination theory and culture (Chirkov et al., 2003). The researchers hypothesized that individuals from four different cultures internalize different cultural practices. Despite these differences, the relative autonomy of individual's motivation for those practices predicted well being in all 4 cultures. The study included 559 people from South Korea, Russia, Turkey, and the United States. Surveys were administered in small groups. Results supported the hypothesized relations between autonomy and well being across cultures and gender (Chirkov et al.). They suggested that, according the self-determination theory, culture is a factor in developing autonomy. An autonomy-supportive environment provides choice, opportunity for self- direction, competence (Deci & Ryan, 1987) and promotes life satisfaction and well being in every human (Ryan & Deci, 2000).

Cultural Factors in Parental Control

According to Cummings, Davies, and Campbell (2000), adolescents are not passive recipients in parent-adolescent relationships. Rather, they are active agents in their own development. Querido, Warner, and Eyberg

(2002) suggested that control and power assertion can be detrimental to the socialization process because it can arouse anger and hostility in the adolescent accompanied by opposition or unwillingness to comply with the parent's wishes. They believed that power assertion also provides a model of aggression that leads to antisocial or immoral conduct. Yet, Bumpus et al (2001) and Chen et al(2000) believed that parents who provide adolescents with responsiveness and independence promote behavioral autonomy.

Several researchers (Boake & Salmon, 2006; Pedersen & Revenson; 2005; Petrocelli, 2003a), suggested that the family environment can have an influence in adolescents' lives. Other researchers (Kowal et al., 2002; McLoyd, Kaplan, Hardaway, & Wood, 2007), contended that parents often interact differently with each child and that discrepancies in parental treatment predict differences in siblings' social and emotional development. For example, a study was conducted with 148 Asian American and White adolescents (Singer & Weinstein, 2000). The study examined the perception of differential affection and control by mother and fathers as predictors of academic achievement and self-perception of intellectual ability and global self worth. Overall results confirmed the hypotheses that the more differentially favorable the treatment (more affection or less control) or the less differential treatment (above and beyond which sibling was favored) reported in the home, the more positive late adolescent outcomes. Mothers were reported to be more controlling of sibling pairs (Singer & Weinstein). Nichols (2005) believed the parent who gets an adolescent to open up is in control of the interaction; "the shift from arguing with a adolescent's protest to hearing him out even drawing him out is a shift from being defensive to taking charge, transforms the whole nature of the relationship" (p. 239). He suggested that parent-adolescent communication is improved leading to greater autonomy.

Other studies on developmental theories conducted by Keener and Boykin (1996) and Pettit, Keiley, Laird, Bates, and Dodge (2007), suggested that parental control comes in different forms and adolescents' adjustment depended on the type of parental control exerted. Control characterized by psychological manipulation was linked with lower levels of adolescent adjustment. Control characterized by parental awareness and involvement in adolescents' activities, efforts to control child's deviance, and low harshness was associated with better adjustment in adolescents (Keener & Boykin). Grotevant and Cooper (1998) believed adolescents do not simply move away from parental influence into a decision-making process of their own. They continue to be connected to parents while moving toward and developing autonomy. According to Patrick, Canevello, Knee, and Lonsbary (2007), the connectedness with parents facilitates the child's social competence and psychological well-being across ethnic groups.

A study examining qualitative differences in parent-adolescent relationships and the risk of externalizing behaviors among Black and Hispanic families showed that Black boys were more assertive than Hispanic boys, who were more passive (Smetana et al.,2000). Black parents were also found to be more autonomy granting and controlling than Hispanic parents. In fact, among the Hispanic families, autonomous behavior was not actively encouraged. Parental control, however, may serve a different function within the context of Black families than Hispanic families. Hispanic families may construe autonomy different than Black families. In other words, behavioral differences and parental control between Black and Hispanic families suggest that culturally derived expectations about the adolescent's development is an important factor in the way it is perceived by the adolescent. Family interactions were examined longitudinally over 2 years in 79 middle-class Black families with young adolescents, mothers and fathers (Smetana et al.). They were videotaped discussing a conflict for 10 minutes. Results showed that mothers' communication in triadic interactions became less positive over time. Both mothers and father's communication was more positive in dyadic than triadic interactions. In triadic interactions, mothers validated sons more than daughters and in dyadic interactions with parents boys were more receptive to parents than were girls Findings from this study suggested Black adolescent parent interactions demonstrate increased autonomy support as children move through adolescence (Smetana et al.).

White families, by comparison, promote individual interest and self-expression (Rothbaum et al., 2000a). Asian families like China promote group interest emphasizing group harmony and social obligation (Rothbaum et al.). White families are also less controlling and encourages choice, thereby, highlighting the adolescents' importance as a family member. Immigrant Chinese families promote relatedness by encouraging inheritance to authority. They reinforce the adolescents' place and security within the family because of other potentially disruptive influences on family cohesion (Rothbaum et al.). In addition, White families emphasize discontinuity of relationships as a way to promote adolescents' independence and freedom to form a nuclear family. According to Lee et al. (2000), immigrant Chinese families emphasize continuity of relationships within the family of origin as fostering the adolescents' independence. Although both groups emphasize independence, on one hand, adolescents may perceive these parental values and beliefs as a threat to developing autonomy and distance themselves from the family. Adolescents may embrace these values because to deny them may disrupt the adolescent's sense of coherence (Lee et al.). They suggested this may be true in regards to Chinese American adolescents whose families strongly value harmony within the family.

Multiple researchers (Camras et el., 2006; Chu, 2007; d'Ailly, 2003), contended that, even though the concept of independence, autonomy, and self-determination are factors influencing adolescents' development, not all cultures enforce these values in the same way. Asian American, Native American, and Latino families may be in conflict with these concepts. They suggested that the Western emphasis on nuclear family and independence could be construed as reducing the importance of the family of origin. For example Sue and Sue (2003) noted that in Chinese American families the notion of loyalty and devotion is a strong determinant of how adolescents behave. Chu suggested that obedience, respect, obligation to parents, and duty leave little room for self-determination and autonomy.

Environmental Factors

Multiple reseachers (Chirkov et al., 2003; Conger et al., 1994; Singer & Weinstein, 2000) suggested that the family environment has an important influence on adolescents' lives. Within cultures, a number of environmental factors impact on a children's development (Gonzales, Pitts, Hill, & Roosa, 2000). They argued that historically, environmental factors such as socioeconomic status have been known to affect ethnic groups in different ways.

Socioeconomic (SES)

Not all ethnic minority families live in poverty (Mandara & Murray, 2000). However, poverty contributes to the well being of all family members who do share this experience (Mandara & Murray; Skowron, 2005). For example, a study examined the effects of martial status, family income, and family functioning on 116, fifteen year old African American adolescents' from various schools in Southern California and their parents (Mandara & Murray). Perceptions of self-esteem and family functioning were obtained from adolescents and parents provided family income and marital status. Fifty percent of the parents were married, 38% were divorced, and 13% were consistently single. Incomes ranged from $5,000 to over $90,000. The Multi-Dimensional Self-Esteem Inventory (MDSEI) was used to measure self-esteem across subscales and the Family Environment Scale (FES) was used to assess perceptions of family environments. Results showed that family functioning was a very strong predictor of self-esteem for boys and girls. However, girls had self-esteem similar to boys when the quality of family functioning was low, but their self-esteem was higher when the quality of family functioning was high. Whereas, boys may be more sensitive to family income, girls may feel more responsible for relationships between family members and their self-esteem is more affected by changes in family functioning than it is for boys (Mandara & Murray). Parents of boys reported a greater emphasis on achievement and competition, control of feelings, and conformity to rules. Girls' parents, on the other hand, reported a greater emphasis on close interpersonal relationships, encouragement to talk about troubles, more frequent physical affection, comfort, and reassurance (Mandara & Murray). Yet, no one asked boys or girls if they believed that talking more to parents about family functioning would enhance self-esteem. This study will extend to previous research by exploring if age and gender differences exist among ethnic groups in adolescents' beliefs of parental support and autonomy development.

Past research also suggested that parents from higher SES backgrounds express a vast amount of warmth and affection toward their adolescents (Chen et al., 2000; Rothbaum et al., 2000a). Likewise, research suggested that parents suffering from economic deprivation and the stress associated with low income or poverty also show nurturance in their relationships with adolescents (Rothbaum et al). There is evidence to suggest that parents from middle or upper income as compared with those from lower SES backgrounds are more likely to promote independence and socialization even in young children (Choo, 2002; Clark & Ladd, 2000; Conger et al., 1994). For example, a study was conducted and family SES was viewed as a potential precursor of both parent-child connectedness and autonomy support (Clark & Ladd). Family SES was expected to correlate positively the both dimensions. The participants included 192 kindergarten children who were part of a large longitudinal study. The children attended schools located in three Midwestern school districts. Informed consent was obtained from parents prior to the children's participation. The sample contained largely two-parent families (78%) that included 36% lower to lower-middle income families (earning $0- $19,999 per year or less), 31% middle-income families ($20,000- 39,999), and 33% middle to upper income families ($40,000 and above). Family Socioeconomic Index scores (SEI; Featherman & Stevens, 1982) averaged 40.65. The ethnicity of the children in the sample was 77% White, 17% were Black, 3% Latino, and 3.5% mixed race or other. Results showed that connectedness was correlated with children's socio emotional orientations, number of mutual friendships, and peer acceptance. The relation between parent-child connectedness and children's peer relationship was mediated by children's pro-social and empathetic orientations. Additional findings of the study showed that parent-child connectedness emerged as an important correlate of children's success in forming friendships and peer group acceptance (Clark & Ladd).

Research showed that across ethnic groups, poverty and economic distress are related to psychological and behavior problems (Chung & Steinberg (2006; Mandara & Murray, 2000; Okazaki, 1997). There are cross-ethnic variations among families regarding how much control is enough and how much autonomy is too much (Cheng & Steinberg). The negative impact appears to be more pronounced among Blacks than among Whites (Pinderhughes et al., 2000). They suggested that struggling families are more prevalent among Mexican Americans. For example, a study examined the relationship between family processes and risk for externalizing behavior problems among urban Black and Hispanic youth (Kim & Ge, 2000). Participants were recruited through the Chicago school system after obtaining parental consent. The sample population consisted of 149 Blacks (58%) and Hispanic (42%) families with boys between ages of 10 and 15. All families were living in poor urban communities. Thirty eight percent of the families reported a total income below $10,000 per year; 74.5% reported an income below 20,000 per year; and 99% reported an income below $30,000 per year. Income level was not evenly distributed across ethnicity; Hispanic families were underrepresented in the lower below $10,000 income group and over-represented in the higher $20000-$30000 income group. As characteristics of the population at large, the percentage of single-parent families vary with it ethnicity; 75% of the Black boys and 34% of the Hispanic boys lived in single-parent homes. The participants were randomly selected from families of inner-city ethnic minority boys at risk for delinquency. Results indicated that high-risk boys were more submissive than low risk boys and when they did assert themselves, high risk boys tended to do so in hostile ways. Parents of high-risk boys were more punitive and less nurturing than parents of low risk boys. Regardless of status, Black boys were more assertive than Hispanic boys and Black parents were less controlling than Hispanic parents (Kim & Ge). With respect to ethnicity and adolescent's autonomy, findings indicated that Black boys were more assertive and separating than Hispanic boys who were more submissive and deferential. Black parents were generally more autonomy granting and less controlling than Hispanic parents. The positive correlation between nurturance /protect and assertive/ trust behavior among Black low risk families suggest that autonomous behavior is more normative and perhaps encouraged within these families when combined with trusting/relying behavior. However, in the Hispanic low risk families a different picture emerged; the positive correlations between authoritarian and punitive parental control practices among low risk Hispanic families suggest that this sort of child behavior is actively discouraged. Similarly, the negative correlation between nurturance /protect and assertive/ trust behavior among the low risk Hispanic families suggested that even what seems to be a mild form of autonomous behavior is not actively encouraged (Kim & Ge). They suggested that these findings complement previous research on the development of antisocial behavior by highlighting the role of the adolescent and family processes.

Stress Factors

Illness within families is a stressful experience for children, particularly parental illness (Pedersen & Revenson, 2005). Research suggested that the effects of parental illness on adolescents can be a potential threat to their development (Kittmer, 2005; Pedersen & Revenson). A study was conducted with a sample of 136 ten year olds and their parents examining the relationship between parent's depressed mood, marital conflict, parent-child hostility, and children's adjustment (Low & Stocker, 2002). They reported that results showed both mothers and fathers depressed mood and marital conflict were associated with adolescent's adjustment problems through disruptions in parent-adolescent relationships.

Negy and Snyder (2006) asserted that environmental stress among families puts children at early risk for learning delays, emotional, and behavioral problems. According to family systems theory, differentiation of self is a central construct on Bowen family systems theory (Bowen, 1988) and is critical to healthy individual development and family functioning. Skowron (2005) believed that, "differentiation of self is the capacity of a system and its members to manage emotional control reactivity, act thoughtfully under stress, and allow for both intimacy and autonomy in relationships" (p. 338).

Another study examined whether family system functioning was associated with resilience in adolescents exposed to negative environmental stress (Skowron, 2005). In a sample of 55 low-income urban families, greater differentiation of self among mothers predicted adolescent competence; better verbal and math achievements scores and decreased aggression after considering the effects of neighborhood violence and family life stress. Results showed that families exposed to substantial rates of neighborhood violence and stressful life events, that is, those mothers who were better at modulating emotions were capable of both intimacy and autonomy demonstrated higher verbal and math achievement scores and were less aggressive (Skowron). In other words, differentiated parents are thought to be more flexible and adaptive because they are able to modulate their emotional responses, maintain a solid sense of self in relationships and their adolescents would learn to think clearly and regulate their emotions (Skowron). He asserted that differentiated parents are more capable of remaining connected with their adolescents while supporting their autonomy. Less differentiated parents are less able to regulate their emotions and find it difficult to remain calm and think clearly in stressful life events which affect adolescents' achievement and behavior.

According to multiple researchers (Cummings et al., 2000; Winters et al., 2006), adolescent maladjustment is commonly rooted in experiences with family discord. Communication between parents and children all ages is integral in how they deal with family discord. Winters et al conducted a study was conducted to examine associations among family discord, caregiver communication quality about emotionally stressful events, and child internal representations of family security. Participants included 50 preschoolers (26 boys and 24 girls) mean age of 4.3 years and their caregivers. Median family income was between $25,000 and $35,000. The sample consisted of 67% Whites, 25 % Blacks, 5% Hispanics and 2% Asians, and 1% other families. Children completed MacArthur Story Stem Battery to measure internal representations. To assess family discord, the FES developed by Moos and Moos (1990) was administered. Results showed that children's representation was predicted by interactions between family discord and caregiver communication quality (Winters et al.). Children exhibiting highest levels of secure representations of the family experienced a consistency between low levels of family discord and communications emphasizing family security. Incongruence between family experiences and communication, reflected in high levels of family discord and communication underscoring family security was associated with the lowest level of children secure representations. Results suggest that child representations depended largely on the fit between caregiver communication quality and family experience. In any event, Skowron (2005) and Winters et al (2006) asserted that ethnicity, culture, and SES are factors determining adolescents' perceptions of their autonomy development. This study represents a further step in research by exploring adolescents' perceptions among four ethnic groups.

Summary

Previous research has focused largely on parents' role in ways they contribute to autonomy development in adolescents. Numerous studies have been conducted gathering data from parents on ways they help adolescents master the environment, meet social demands, and ultimately developing autonomy. Communication, rules, parental support, expression of views, and having input into family decisions, are factors that influence autonomy development. Studies asking adolescents how they perceive these factors as determining their autonomy development have been largely ignored. Parents play a very significant role in their adolescents' life. There are times when parents must rely on adolescents for information, particularly when they are outside the home. This gap in knowledge is a particular concern considering adolescents have rights to opinions and they do have knowledge and insight into factors that affect their autonomy development.

Adolescent are keen observers, not only visually but also through all the other senses. On the basis of these observations adolescents interpret, perceive, and figure out things in their own way. Even though they have not yet acquired the adult form of sensing, reasoning, and responding, this does not diminish the soundness and significance of adolescents' perceptions and interpretations (Stepp, 2000). Adolescents, like adults, should have a voice and input into decisions that affect them most directly (Harter et al., 1998; Melton, 1996). While interacting with family members, particularly parents, adolescents need opportunities to share their perceptions and views on situations and events that occur in their lives. Lack of parental support and opportunities for self-expression also presents high risk of additional problems. Some of these problems are experiencing emotions such as shame, guilt, anger, frustration, feeling unimportant, unaccepted, no self-worth or importance in the family, withdrawal, low self-esteem, and social problems. Lack of parental support to express views and communicate could also lead adolescents to become vulnerable to negative peer influence as a means of feeling accepted by others. Perceptions of irrelevance and lack of parental support to develop autonomy could also place adolescents at very high risk of engaging in behaviors leading to juvenile justice system involvement. If adolescents perceive that parents are listening, supportive, encouraging, and receptive to their views and comments, this is likely to have a significant impact on developing autonomy. What counts most is the meaning adolescents assign to a given experience (d'Ailly, 2000; Davalos et al., 2005; Yamamoto, 1993). This study is needed to examine factors that determine and influence adolescents' perceptions of their autonomy development.

Across cultures and among ethnic groups, children all ages want a chance to feel worthwhile and respected as a person and a human being worthy of dignity (Hart, 1991b, Melton, 1996; 2005a). Although values and beliefs differ in some ways among ethnic groups, there is a concept of autonomy in all groups. For example, in some groups, autonomy may be in the form of unity and dependence within the family. Among other groups autonomy may be encouraged in children and adolescents by means of open communication, taking initiative, and learning ways to be more independent (Murphy-Berman et al., 1996; Winters et al., 2006). Autonomy is also influenced by environmental factors such as socioeconomic status. Low income parents may encourage early autonomy among their adolescents due to shortage of resources and financial strain. On the other hand, middle income parents may be better able to provide autonomy support and involvement for adolescents (Rothbaum et al., 2000a; Skowron, 2005).

According to family systems theory, each member of a family has learned a role that characterizes his or her behavior. Parents serve as natural leaders of families. All members in the family have a voice and can speak for themselves (Satir & Bitters, 2000). Stepp (2000) and Yamamato (1993) believed that given the opportunity, adolescents can communicate their views and possibly increase parent's understanding of their world as they see it. Multiple researchers (Davalos et al., 2005: Ryan & Deci; 2000; Satir

& Whitaker, 2000) contended that parents can enhance each adolescent's autonomy by listening, acknowledging, appreciating, and remaining receptive to what the child has to say.

The purpose of this study was to explore factors determining adolescent's perceptions of ways they develop autonomy. This study will extend to other studies by exploring factors determining adolescents' perceptions of parental support and parent-adolescent communication style. This study also adds to previous research by examining the perceptions of four ethnic groups of children. Chapter 3 includes a description of the research design and methodology, setting and sample, justification for this approach, instrumentation, data collection, research questions, hypotheses, and analysis, and ethical consideration of this study.

CHAPTER 3: METHODOLOGY

Introduction

The purpose of this study was to examine the relationships between perceptions of parental support as measured by the POPS, adolescent-parent communication as measured by the PACS, and the autonomy development as measured by the RAI. The relationships between these variables were examined by implementing descriptive statistics, correlation analysis, multiple regression analysis and MANOVA. This chapter includes a description of this study's design, sample, instrumentation, data analysis, and ethical considerations. An overview of the study's design will include a rationale for why this particular research design was selected. The sample characteristics and size is presented as well as a description of the instrumentation. The data collection and analysis will also be explained.

Purpose of the Study

The purpose of this study was to examine factors determining adolescents' perceptions of ways they develop autonomy. This study does so by examining adolescents' beliefs about whether they have parental support to express their views and thereby, develop greater autonomy. For the sake of this study, views include communication, expressing opinions and ideas, having voice, sharing personal experiences, and input into family decisions and discussions. Parents include natural parents, adoptive parents, stepparents, and legal guardians. This study further examined whether differences exist among adolescent's autonomy development based on ethnicity. Finally, this study examined whether age and gender differences exist among adolescents and autonomy development. Ethnic groups used in this study were Asians, Blacks, Hispanics, and Whites.

Research Design and Approach

This study was quantitative in nature. It was non experimental, descriptive, and correlational. It was non-experimental because changes or interventions were not introduced in the study (Polit & Hunger, 1999). This study was descriptive because it described patterns. This study was correlational because it examined relationships between variables such as parental support, parent-adolescent communication, and autonomy (Polit & Hunger, 1999). Ethnicity, gender, and age were demographic variables in this study. Correlation does not prove causation as the mere existence of relationships. Even strong ones are not enough to warrant the conclusion that one variable caused the other (Polit & Hungler, 1999). Therefore, this study was not meant to say that perceptions among adolescents determine autonomy. Rather, this study examined adolescents' perceptions of their autonomy development. Therefore, this quantitative non experimental design allows for discovery of new knowledge of the interrelationships among these variables.

Multiple variables exist in this study (i.e. autonomy, parental support, and parent-adolescent communication) making multiple regression analysis appropriate for this study design. By using multiple regression analysis one is able to determine the impact several predictor variables have on a single criterion variable in the model. MANOVA was also implemented in this study in order to determine the impact the demographic variables (race and gender) have on all of the scores received from the surveys (Hand & Taylor, 1987; Moore & McCabe, 2004).

Setting and Sample

This study consisted of 130 participants from four ethnic groups. This includes 27 Asians, 35 Blacks, 32 Hispanics, 33 Whites, and 3 Biracial students of which 72 were girls and 58 were boys. Based on a medium effect size (.15) at a .05 alpha level, and 80% power, which are standard for research studies (Cohen, 1992), as well as a total of 8 predictor variables in the model, a minimum total of 109 participants are required for the variables in this study. This information was obtained by using the tables and suggestions made by Cohen (1992) in his article on statistical power analysis and the sample size estimating program G*Power.

The participants included 6th, 7th, and 8th graders attending 2 different middle schools throughout nearby communities. In these communities 6th through 8th grade levels consist of middle school students based on the school districts' description. Participants met the adolescent age group. The school district and community consist of a diversity of children with varying ethnic backgrounds. Their grade levels provide them with the necessary reading comprehension skills to complete questionnaires with the researcher's assistance as needed. Ethnicity was determined by the participant, parent, or guardian.

Statistical analysis determined that this study would require a minimum sample of at least 109 participants (Cohen, 1992). Brief background information on the study, the procedures for participation, a discussion of confidentiality, anonymity, child/parent informed consent, the voluntary nature of the study, and ethical concerns was provided.

Individuals who indicated that they were in agreement to the conditions for participation in the study completed the permission granted scales and questionnaires. The researcher was available for assistance as needed.

The questionnaires were all administered and completed in school during one interval at an agreed upon time with the principals. The researcher was available during test administration to assist as needed. Otherwise, time was allowed for participants to complete the tests on their own. Participant's personal information such as name, gender, and age was de-identified and coded on each test by the researcher. A brief demographic questionnaire collected information about the participant's ethnicity, age, gender, and parental information.

Instrumentation and Materials

The Relative Autonomy Index (RAI) of the Self-Regulation Questionnaire-Academic developed by Ryan and Connell (1989) was used in this study to measure autonomy. The scale was developed for children in late elementary and middle school. This scale was developed as a concept of the self-determination theory (SDT). It differentiates types of behavioral regulation in terms of the degree of autonomous or self-determined functioning. The scale consists of 32 items with responses on a 4-point scale ranging from very true to not at all true.

Validity and reliability of the SRQ-A was tested in a study assessing three dimensions of parent styles; autonomy support, involvement, and provisions of structure in 64 mothers and 50 fathers of elementary school children grades 3-6 (Grolnick & Ryan, 1989). Items For mother ratings, reliabilities ranged from .71 (information) to .78 (autonomy techniques) with an average of .75. For fathers, reliabilities ranged from .75 to .84 with an average of .80. Discrepancies were evenly distributed through the five points on the scale. Results indicated that for both mothers and fathers there were no gender effects on either the involvement or structure dimensions. However, significant gender effects emerged on the autonomy-support dimension indicating that mothers, F (1, 62) = 10.70, p <.001, and fathers F (1, 48) = 4.05, p <.05, were more autonomy-supportive with girls than with boys. There were no significant effects for grade level. Construct validity data for this study suggested that the three parent dimensions were reliable, relatively independent, and correlated with other parent measures of autonomy (Grolnick & Ryan, 1989).

The Perception of Parent Scale, developed by Grolnick et al., (1991), was used in this study to measure perceptions of parent support. The POPS is a questionnaire developed to assess concepts of the self-determination theory (SDT) (Grolnick et al., 1991; Ryan & Deci, 2000). The POPS is used to measure children's perception of the degree to which their parents are autonomy supportive and controlling in their approach to parenting. The test is used for ages 8 and older. The scales are completed by children to describe their mothers and their fathers. The scales consist of 22 items, 11 mother items and then the same 11 items for fathers. These items of form an autonomy support subscale for each parent and an involvement of subscale for each parent.

Because the scale is used with children as young as age 8 years old and often in classroom settings, the children respond right on the questionnaire by circling a letter in front of the one (out of four) description of a parent that is most like their own parent. Each item gives two opposite statements describing parents as either involved or not involved, or as either autonomy supportive or controlling. The child chooses one of the two descriptions that best describe his or her parents, and then decides whether the statement is "sort of true" or "really true" of his or her parent (Grolnick et al., 1991).

The reliability of the scale has been shown to be internally consistent with Cronbach's alpha ranging from .55 to .70 (Cronbach et al., 1991). Thus, the hypotheses, parents who are less controlling and high in autonomy support would allow their children to develop a sense of themselves as locus of initiation of their actions, thereby, promoting more perceived autonomy and control understanding (outcomes). The internal consistency coefficient for this scale is .68. Validity: Test retest reliability comparisons were directly related to provide additional support that the scale is a valid measure (Grolnick et al., 1991).

A study on the reliability and validity of the POPS was conducted by Wintre, Gallander, Yaffe, and Marvin (1991). The study measured the transformation in parent-child relations from the initial positions of authority and obedience to the mature position of mutual reciprocity (Wintre et al., 1991). A 51-item, 4-point Likert scale was designed. Items were divided into three classes dealing with relationships with parents, mothers, and fathers. The scale was administered to 132 university students (85 females, 47 males), 18-25 years old. Consultant choice, self-esteem, and locus of control were employed to examine construct validity. Cronbach alpha on a reduced scale of 43 items indicated a reliable measure 43-item scale.

Factor analysis of the scale yielded three interpretable factors. There was no significant sex difference for scale scores. A one-way ANOVA using median split on the POPS scores revealed that students with transformed relationships were more likely that other children to choose adults as consultants, had higher self-esteem, and were less likely to attribute circumstances to powerful others (Wintre et al., 1991). Thus, the POPS scale appears to be reliable and the construct validity indicators confirmed the hypothesis that that was a positive correlation between self-esteem and POPS scores (Wintre et al., 1991).

The Parent Adolescent Communication Scale developed by Barnes and Olson (1982) was used in this study to measure parent adolescent communication style. This scale can be used to assess attitudes and open family communication in parent-child relationships. It is for ages 12 and older. The PACS is a paper-pencil test. There are 20 items on a five-point scale, ranging from 1 = strongly agree to 5 = strongly disagree. The scale is divided into two subscales (10 items each) measuring two dimensions: Openness and Problems.

The first subscale, Openness, focuses on the free-flowing exchange of information, both factual and emotional, as well as on the perception of the lack of constraint and the degree of understanding and satisfaction experienced in the interaction. Examples of items from this subscale include: "My father/mother/child is always a good listener. When I ask questions, I get honest answers from my father/mother/child." The second subscale, Problems, focuses on the negative aspects of communication such as the hesitancy to share, or selectively and caution in what is shared, and negative styles of interaction. Examples of items measuring the existence of problems in communication are, "There are topics I avoid discussing with my father/mother/child. I don't think I can tell my father/mother/child how I really feel about some things." Adolescents are requested to assess communication with their mothers and fathers separately (Barnes & Olson, (1982).

Alpha reliabilities for each subscale are .87 and .78; test-retest reliabilities are .78 and .77. A study on the validation of the PACS was conducted to assess adolescent girls' frequency of sexual communication with their parents (Sales, Milhausen, Wingood, DiClemente, Salazar, & Crosby, 2002). The PACS was administered to 522 African American female adolescents ranging from ages 14 to 18. Internal consistency of the PACS (Cronbach's alpha) was .88 at baseline, .89 at the 6 month follow up assessment, and .90 at the 12 month follow up assessment.

Test retest reliability between baseline and 6 month follow up scores was significant (r = .58, p<.001), indicated good reliability. Concurrent construct validity was correlated significantly with other measures being positively associated with frequency of sexual communication, partner, family support, and perceived parental knowledge. Discriminant and predictive construct validity was significantly correlated in the predicted direction. Results of this study indicate that the PACS is a reliable and valid measure of frequency of sexual communication between female adolescent and their parents (Sales et al., 2006). This is a utilized scale in the family communication (Barnes & Olson, 1982; Sales, 2006).

Reliability and validity of the PACS was also used to assess family functioning and communication in another study (Bhushan & Ravi, 1988). Data from 100 Indian male University students in Northern India was used to assess the construct validity and reliability of the PACS and the family Adaptability and Cohesion Evaluation Scale III. Both measures were found to be reliable and valid (Bhushan & Ravi, 1988).

Data Collection and Analysis

This study used several statistical procedures to answer research questions and test hypotheses. The Correlation Matrix was used to analyze correlation between the predictor variables with the Pearson Product Moment coefficient. Multiple Regression analysis was used to examine relationships between the continuously distributed variables of the POPS and PACS as well as the discrete variables of gender and race. A MANOVA was used to examine the impacts the race and gender of the students had on the scores obtained on the PACS, POPS and SRQ-A.

Descriptive statistics were calculated for each one of the variables in the model. These included the calculation of frequency tables that provide information on the number and percentage of observations that make up each one of the categories for that variable. Summary statistics were also calculated for the continuous variables in the model. This includes calculating the mean, standard deviation, minimum, maximum, skewness and kurtosis statistics. The skewness and kurtosis statistics were used to illustrate the distribution of the variables and whether or not they are non-normal.

Research Question 1: Is there a relationship between an adolescent's autonomy development and perceptions of parental support and parent-adolescent communication style? It is proposed that there was a positive correlation between adolescent's autonomy development and perceptions of parental support and parent-adolescent communication style. In other words, the more positive are the perceptions, the greater the autonomy.

Null Hypothesis 1: There was no significant relationship between adolescent's autonomy development as measured by the RAI of the SRQ-A and the variables of perception of parental support as measured by the POPS, and adolescent-parent communication as measured by the PACS.

Alternative Hypotheses 1: There is a significant relationship between measures of autonomy development as measured by the RAI of the SRQ-A and the variables of perception of parental support as measured by the POPS, and adolescent-parent communication as measured by the PACS.

Question 1 was first addressed by using the Correlation matrix between the predictor variables of the model. The reason for this was to determine whether there was a significant relationship between the predictor variables which would result in confounding variables (Moore & McCabe, 2004). A Correlation matrix describes correlation among variables. It is a square symmetrical matrix with the element equal to the correlation coefficient. Correlation coefficient indicates the degree of linear relationship between two variables and always lies between -1 and +1. Correlation depends on comparing two distributions of scores. Negative (- or decrease) and positive (+ or increase) signs in correlation are only used to suggest direction (Keith, 2005; Rudestam & Newton, 2001). For example, as X increases, Y decreases denotes a negative correlation and as X increases, Y increases denotes a positive correlation. Other studies that explored relationships between parental and peer support have used the Correlation Matrix and Pearson Product moment correlation coefficient to analyze data ((Damrad, 2007; Holder, 2002; Liebert, 1998; Snuggs, 2007).

In order to determine whether there was a significant relationship between the POPS, PACS scores, and the RAI scores as measured by the SRQ-A a multiple regression analysis was implemented. By using a multiple regression model to test this hypothesis one is able to fit several predictor variables to the model at the same time. This was done to examine whether the individual predictor variable has a positive impact on the dependent variable while accounting for the other variables included in the model. This, in effect, allows one to examine the relationships between several predictor variables and one dependent variable at the same time (Moore & McCabe, 2004).

To determine the optimal set, simultaneous and stepwise regression is frequently used to explore and maximize predictors (Petrocelli, 2003a). Stepwise regression involves determining and removing variables from the regression equation based on correlation statistics (Petrocelli, 2003a). Again, both of the statistical procedures are appropriate and have been used in family environment studies (Kittmer, 2005; Petrocelli, 2003b; Querido, Warner, & Eyberg, 2002).

Research Question 2: Can adolescents' autonomy development be predicted by their perceptions of parental support and parent-adolescent communication and demographic variables of age and gender?

Null Hypotheses 2: Perceptions of parental support as measured by the POPS and adolescent-parent communication as measured by the PACS and the demographic variables of age and gender will not each independently account for a significant portion of the variance in autonomy development as measured by the RAI of the SRQ-A.

Alternative Hypothesis 2: Perceptions of parental support as measured by the POPS and adolescent-parent communication as measured by the PACS and the demographic variables of age and gender will each independently account for a significant portion of the variance in autonomy development as measured by the RAI of the SRQ-A.

Question 2 was analyzed using Multiple Regression analysis. This is a multivariate statistical technique that examines relationships between continuously distributed independent variables (parental support and parent-adolescent communication) and one continuously distributed dependent variable (autonomy) (Rudestam & Newton, 2001). Multiple Regression is reported to be a strong set of methods for analyzing specific hypotheses and relationships among experimental, quasi-experimental, and non-experimental data (Petrocelli, 2003a). This statistical procedure is appropriate for exploratory studies.

Research Question 3: Are there ethnic group and gender differences in adolescents' autonomy development, perceptions of parental support, family environment, and parent-communication?

Null Hypotheses 3: There are no significant differences in beliefs among ethnic groups and by gender of autonomy development as measures by the RAI of the SRQ-A, perceptions of parental support as measured by the POPS, and adolescent-parent communication as measured by the PACS.

Alternative Hypotheses 3: There are significant differences in beliefs among ethnic groups and by gender of autonomy development as measures by the RAI of the SRQ-A, perceptions of parental support as measured by the POPS, and adolescent-parent communication as measured by the PACS.

Question 3 was assessed by implementing an MANOVA. The use of the MANOVA is most appropriate in situations when there are multiple dependent or criterion variables in the model (Hand & Taylor, 1987). This was appropriate for question three because there are several dependent variables that consist of scores from the RAI as measured by the SRQ-A, the POPS scores and the PACS scores. The predictor variables for this question are the gender and race of the students in the study.

An advantage of the MANOVA is that it allows one to account for the extra variability that may exist between the criterion variables, since the measurements are collected from the same individual (Hand & Taylor,

1987). Because the criterion variables were collected from the same participant, several different two-way ANOVAs would not be appropriate for the analysis, since they would not be able to account for the extra variability in the model. For this reason, there would be a higher chance of making type II errors when it comes to the interpretations of the results (Hand & Taylor, 1987).

The questionnaires were hand scored. The SPSS 16.0 Software Package (2006) was used to perform statistics and analyze data. The SPSS 16.0 analyses includes graphs, statistical performance of t-tests, analysis of variance and covariance, measures of linear regression and correlation, multiple regression, multi-way frequency analysis, discriminant analysis, logistic regression, and factor analysis. Details of ways to perform nonparametric tests are also included in the SPSS 16.0 software package (Carver, 2006; Spiegel & Stepens, 2004).

Ethical Protection of Participants

Consideration was given to the nature of this study and its possible effects on the participants. Informed consent parent / child assent forms were distributed to all potential participants discussing the procedures for participating in the study, confidentiality issues, the volunteer nature of the study, minimal to no risk, and a way to contact the researcher with individual questions regarding this study. It was clearly stated in the informed consent that all records in this study will remain confidential and only the researcher will have access to those records.

Personal information was de-identified and replaced with codes only accessible to the researcher. Potential participants were notified that they were free to withdraw for the study at any time during the process without consequences. Additionally, their decision as to whether or not to participate in this study would not in any way affect their relationship in the school, district or community. There were no physical risks or benefits for participation in the study other than greater self-awareness. However, there was the potential for minimal risk for emotional upset as participants reflected on self-development. Participants were notified that there is no obligation to complete any part of the study in which they feel uncomfortable.

Summary

This chapter included the research design, methodology, and data collection and analysis. Chapter 4 of this study is structured around the research questions and hypotheses. Chapter 4 will address the actual study and findings. Chapter 5 will provide a brief overview explaining how and why the study was conducted. A summary of findings and relation to the research questions and hypotheses will also be provided in chapter 5.

CHAPTER 4: RESULTS

Introduction

The objective of this chapter is to discuss the results from the statistical analyses conducted to address the objectives of this study. In order to address the objectives of this study, this chapter is divided up into four different sections; summary statistics, results for hypotheses 1, results for hypotheses 2, and results for hypotheses 3. Summary statistics are presented for each one of the items included in the study. This includes calculating the mean, standard deviation, minimum and maximum values as well as the skewness and kurtosis measurements. The summary section also includes frequency tables that illustrate the occurrence of each one of the discrete variables in the model.

In order to address the first hypothesis, a multiple regression analysis was conducted since there are a number of different variables that were going to be compared with the dependent variable of the autonomy development as measured by the RAI. By using a multiple regression model one is able to compare the impact a number of different independent variables have on a dependent variable at the same time. This is more appropriate than a correlation coefficient since one is able to account for the other variables in the model when interpreting the size of effect the variable has on the dependent variable.

Hypothesis 2 of this study was to determine whether there is a significant relationship between the RAI score and the perceptions of parental support as measured by the POPS, adolescent-parent communication as measured by the PACS, the age and gender of the child. Once again, this is accomplished by conducting a multiple regression analysis.

The final hypothesis is examined by using a MANOVA which allows one to determine the impact a number of different independent variables have on several dependent variables that come from the same subject. For this reason, the MANOVA is appropriate for this hypothesis since the researcher is assessing whether there is a significant relationship between the child's gender and ethnicity when it comes to the three measurements of the adolescents' autonomy development, perceptions of parental support, and parent-communication (Hand & Taylor, 1997). This is more appropriate than conducting a number of ANOVA tables since there would be a greater chance of observing a type II error because the dependent variables are related to one another.

Descriptive Statistics

The first set of results illustrated in the analysis is the frequency distributions of each one of the demographic variables. Table 1 presents the results for the distribution of the age of the participants in the study. The highest percentage of participants in the study was 13 years of age (30.8%). This was followed by participants that were 14 years old (24.6%) and participants that were 11 and 12 (20% each). It can also be seen from the table that there were only 2 participants were 10.5 years old while there was only four participants that were 10 years old. Because there were so few participants in these last two age categories, they were combined to form a group that consisted of participants under the age of 11.

Table 1
Age of Participants

		Frequency	Percent	Valid Percent	Cumulative Percent
Valid	10	4	3.1	3.1	3.1
	10.5	2	1.5	1.5	4.6
	11	26	20.0	20.0	24.6
	12	26	20.0	20.0	44.6
	13	40	30.8	30.8	75.4
	14	32	24.6	24.6	100.0
	Total	130	100.0	100.0	

The grade level for each of the participants is presented in Table 2. Table 2 illustrates that that a higher percentage of participants were in the 6th grade (38.5%) while the fewest came from the 8th grade (26.2%). There was a total of 46 participants that were in grade seven which made up 35.4% of the observations.

Table 2
Grade Level of Participants

		Frequency	Percent	Valid Percent	Cumulative Percent
Valid	6	50	38.5	38.5	38.5
	7	46	35.4	35.4	73.8
	8	34	26.2	26.2	100.0
	Total	130	100.0	100.0	

In Table 3, the self-reported race of the participants are illustrated. The highest percentage of participants in the study was Black (26.9%). This was closely followed by participants that were White (25.4%) and participants that were Hispanic (24.6%). There were only 3 participants that noted Bi-racial. Because there were not many participants in this group, they were removed from the study. This is because there would not be sufficient data in order to calculate a mean score for these individuals.

Table 3
Participants Self Reported Race

		Frequency	Percent	Valid Percent	Cumulative Percent
Valid	Asian	27	20.8	20.8	20.8
	Black	35	26.9	26.9	47.7
	Hispanic	32	24.6	24.6	72.3
	White	33	25.4	25.4	97.7
	Bi-racial	3	2.3	2.3	100.0
	Total	130	100.0	100.0	

The results in Table 4 show that over half of the students in this study were female (55.4%).

Table 4
Gender of Participants

		Frequency	Percent	Valid Percent	Cumulative Percent
Valid	Female	72	55.4	55.4	55.4
	Male	58	44.6	44.6	100.0
	Total	130	100.0	100.0	

Table 5 presents the frequencies for the participant's parents' education. A total of 46 participants had parents who had a high school (HS) or GED education (35.4%). This was closely followed by parents with some college (26.9%) and college graduate (26.9%). There were also 2 missing values for the education.

Table 5

Parental Education

		Frequency	Percent	Valid Percent	Cumulative Percent
Valid	Less than HS	12	9.2	9.4	9.4
	HS or GED	46	35.4	35.9	45.3
	Some College	35	26.9	27.3	72.7
	College Grad	35	26.9	27.3	100.0
	Total	128	98.5	100.0	
Missing	System	2	1.5		
Total		130	100.0		

Presented in Table 6 is the income of the participant's parents. Of the participants in the study, 56 had parents that had an income between 20k and 49k (43.1%). This was closely followed by 50+ (30.8%). There were also 3 missing values for the income.

Table 6

Parental Income

		Frequency	Percent	Valid Percent	Cumulative Percent
Valid	0-19k	31	23.8	24.4	24.4
	20-49k	56	43.1	44.1	68.5
	50+	40	30.8	31.5	100.0
	Total	127	97.7	100.0	
Missing	System	3	2.3		
Total		130	100.0		

The results in the following table present the summary statistics for each one of the items on the surveys. Based on the results of the skewness and kurtosis values, there does not appear to be much concern for non normality in the data since most of the scores are relatively small (less than 1 or less than three standard deviations from zero) (Spiegel & Stephens, 1999). This is important because this illustrates that the data follows a normal distribution and therefore allows one to use statistical analyses based on the assumptions of normality.

Table 7
Skewness and Kurtosis analysis

	N	Minimum	Maximum	Mean	Std. Deviation	Skewness		Kurtosis	
	Statistic	Statistic	Statistic	Statistic	Statistic	Statistic	Std. Error	Statistic	Std. Error
SRQ-A External Regulation	130	1.78	4.00	3.1427	.42916	-.372	.212	.428	.422
SRQ-A Introjected Regulation	130	1.11	4.00	2.4393	.73114	.030	.212	-.719	.422
SRQ-A Identified Regulation	130	1.00	4.00	3.0725	.65217	-.697	.212	.125	.422
SRQ-A Intrinsic Motivation	130	1.00	4.00	2.6275	.77810	-.257	.212	-.601	.422
SRQ-A Relative Autonomy Index (RAI)	130	-5.11	2.76	-.3973	1.57380	-.298	.212	-.234	.422
POPS Mother Involvement	130	1.00	4.00	3.0600	.73396	-.836	.212	.289	.422
POPS Mother Autonomy Support	130	1.00	3.17	2.0205	.59027	-.179	.212	-.996	.422
POPS Father Involvement	130	1.00	4.00	2.5200	.71250	-.506	.212	-.297	.422
POPS Father Autonomy Support	130	1.00	3.33	2.0513	.64761	-.176	.212	-1.039	.422
Parent-Adolescent Communication: Mother	130	20.00	100.00	67.5923	17.03971	-.448	.212	.013	.422
Parent-Adolescent Communication: Father	130	22.00	100.00	61.6154	16.74912	-.021	.212	-.403	.422
Valid N (listwise)	130								

The participants in this study were diverse across age, gender, income and race. These middle school students ranged in ages from less than 11 years of age to 14 years of age with the largest group represented by 13 year olds. The parents of the student were largely from a middle class background. 35.4% of the parents reported having an education that was at a high school level or GED, while 43.1% had an income that was between $20,000 and $49,000.

Data Analysis and Findings

Hypothesis 1

There will be no significant relationship between adolescent's autonomy development as measured by the RAI of the SRQ-A and the variables of perception of parental support as measured by the POPS and adolescent-parent communication as measured by the PACS.

This hypothesis is addressed by performing a multiple regression analysis on the variables desired to be examined. These include the scores on the POPS and PACS instruments as predictor variables and the RAI as the criterion variable. In order to address the chances of there being confounding variables in the model a correlation matrix of the independent variables is produced. Confounding variables occur in model when the independent variables in the model are not independent of one another (Keuhl, 2000). In other words, they are related to both the dependent and independent variables. The results of the correlation can be seen in the following table. As shown in Table 8, several of the variables are in fact correlated with one another. To account for this correlation between the independent variables a stepwise regression method was used to select the variables to include in the model. The stepwise selection method starts by placing the variable that has the smallest p-value into the model. This process is then repeated for each one of the other variables until either they are all in the model or they do not meet the entry criteria which is determined at the start of the analysis. For this study the entry criteria were that the p-value was less than 0.05.

When a variable that is in the model is found to be no longer significant based on a removal criteria, then it is removed from the model. The removal criteria for this study was set equal to 0.10 so that if a p-value fell above this value when all the other variables were included in the model then it would be removed. This helps in preventing confounding variables as well. The result of the stepwise selection method is illustrated in Table 9.

Table 8

Correlation analysis between the scores on the POPS and PACS instruments

		POPS Mother Involvement	POPS Mother Autonomy Support	POPS Father Involvement	POPS Father Autonomy Support	Parent-Adolescent Communication: Mother	Parent-Adolescent Communication: Father
POPS Mother Involvement	Pearson Correlation	1.000	.467**	.339**	.057	.689**	.299**
	Sig. (2-tailed)		.000	.000	.523	.000	.001
	N	130.000	130	130	130	130	130
POPS Mother Autonomy Support	Pearson Correlation	.467**	1.000	.371**	.216*	.503**	.376**
	Sig. (2-tailed)	.000		.000	.013	.000	.000
	N	130	130.000	130	130	130	130
POPS Father Involvement	Pearson Correlation	.339**	.371**	1.000	.262**	.362**	.623**
	Sig. (2-tailed)	.000	.000		.003	.000	.000
	N	130	130	130.000	130	130	130
POPS Father Autonomy Support	Pearson Correlation	.057	.216*	.262**	1.000	.118	.410**
	Sig. (2-tailed)	.523	.013	.003		.181	.000
	N	130	130	130	130.000	130	130
Parent-Adolescent Communication: Mother	Pearson Correlation	.689**	.503**	.362**	.118	1.000	.461**
	Sig. (2-tailed)	.000	.000	.000	.181		.000
	N	130	130	130	130	130.000	130
Parent-Adolescent Communication: Father	Pearson Correlation	.299**	.376**	.623**	.410**	.461**	1.000
	Sig. (2-tailed)	.001	.000	.000	.000	.000	
	N	130	130	130	130	130	130.000

**. Correlation is significant at the 0.01 level (2-tailed).
*. Correlation is significant at the 0.05 level (2-tailed).

Table 9 illustrates that the variables that were kept in the model were the POPS mother autonomy group (p-value = 0.001) and the PAC father measurement (p-value = 0.03). Since these were both found to be significant this would mean that for the POPS variable, the model would predict that for every unit increase in the Mother Autonomy Support the RAI will increase by 0.755 units, after accounting for the PAC father variable. Similarly, the model would predict that for every unit increase in PAC father the RAI will increase by 0.025 units, after accounting for the POPS variable. Since both of the coefficients are positive and significant this means that they both have a positive relationship with the RAI scores.

Gloria D. Fondren, Ph.D.

Table 9
Final fitted model after the stepwise selection method

Model		Unstandardized Coefficients		Standardized Coefficients			95% Confidence Interval for B	
		B	Std. Error	Beta	t	Sig.	Lower Bound	Upper Bound
	(Constant)	-3.444	.548		-6.284	.000	-4.528	-2.359
	POPS Mother Autonomy Support	.755	.228	.283	3.316	.001	.304	1.205
	Parent-Adolescent Communication: Father	.025	.008	.263	3.077	.003	.009	.041

a. Dependent Variable: SRQ-A Relative Autonomy Index (RAI)
b. R-Square = 0.205

The R^2 for the model selected using the stepwise selection method was equal to 0.205. This means that the POPS Mother Autonomy Support and the Parent-Adolescent Communication: Father variables explain 20% of the variation in the SRQ-A Relative Autonomy Index.

Hypothesis 2

Perceptions of parental support as measured by the POPS and adolescent-parent communication as measured by the PACS and the demographic variables of age and gender will not each independently account for a significant portion of the variance in autonomy development as measured by the RAI of the SRQ-A.

To address this hypothesis a multiple regression model was fit with the predictor variables being the POPS and PACS as well as the age and gender of the child. The criterion variable was the RAI score. In previous analyses it was found that several of the POPS and PACS variables are significantly related to one another. It was also found that only two if the variables were significantly related to the RAI score. Because of this, only the two variables found to be significant in the previous analysis are included in this model along with the age and gender of the student. The results of this regression analysis are presented in the following table.

Table 10

ANOVA of variance results for the regression of POPS and PACS as well as the age and gender on the RAI scores.

Source	Type III Sum of Squares	df	Mean Square	F	Sig.
Corrected Model	68.402[a]	4	17.101	8.513	.000
Intercept	4.108	1	4.108	2.045	.155
gender2	.462	1	.462	.230	.632
pops_mas	22.477	1	22.477	11.189	.001
pac_fath	19.285	1	19.285	9.600	.002
Age	2.542	1	2.542	1.265	.263
Error	251.109	125	2.009		
Total	340.033	130	Delete		
Corrected Total	319.512	129			

a. R Squared = .214

Table 11

Parameter estimates for the regression of POPS and PACS as well as the age and gender on the RAI scores.

Parameter	B	Std. Error	t	Sig.	95% Confidence Interval	
					Lower Bound	Upper Bound
Intercept	-2.074	1.412	-1.470	.144	-4.868	.719
[gender2=1]	.121	.252	.480	.632	-.378	.620
[gender2=2]	0[a]	.	.	.	.	.
pops_mas	.765	.229	3.345	.001	.312	1.218
pac_fath	.025	.008	3.098	.002	.009	.041
Age	-.118	.105	-1.125	.263	-.325	.089

Based on the results presented in Table 11 the age and gender did not have a significant effect on the scores of the RAI (p-value = 0.263 and 0.632, respectively). The POPS Mother Autonomy and PAC father scores, however, are still significant. Since these were both found to be significant this would mean that for the POPS variable, the model would predict that for every unit increase in the Mother Autonomy Support the RAI will increase by 0.229 units, after accounting for the other variables in the model. Similarly, the model would predict that every unit increase in PAC father the RAI will increase by 0.008 units, after accounting for the other variables in the model. Both of the coefficients for the POPS and PAC scores are positive and significant. This means that they both have a positive relationship with the RAI scores. This does not provide any evidence against the null hypothesis for the age and gender of the student explaining a significant portion of the variation in RAI though. The model was found to have an R^2 value of 0.214 meaning that the inclusion of age and gender only explained approximately 1% of the variation in RAI scores.

Hypothesis 3

There are no significant differences in beliefs among ethnic groups and by gender of autonomy development as measured by the RAI of the SRQ-A, perceptions of parental support as measured by the POPS, and adolescent-parent communication as measured by the PACS.

The MANOVA would be appropriate for this study because it allows one to model a number of different response variables from the same participant to a number of different independent variables at the same time. This is a better approach than the univariate ANOVA approach since the responses from each participant may be correlated with one another (Hand & Taylor, 1987). It is this correlation that the univariate ANOVA would not be able to account for. This is because the ANOVA assumes that each observation is independent of one another. Because of this mis-interpretations could be made on the independent variables because of the extra variability in the model.

By using the MANOVA you are able to account for this extra variability by using a different covariance structure which accounts for the relationship between the dependent variables. In this case, the dependent variables are the SRQ-A, POPS, and PACS. Because these measurements are taken from each one of the participants it would be assumed that the results obtained from each one of the tests would be highly correlated with one another when the results come form a single participant. The independent variables in this case would be the gender and ethnicity of the participant.

The results for this analysis are presented in Table 12 below. This table shows that the race of the child has a significant effect on the several of the dependent variables. For instance, race is found to be significantly related to the RAI scores (p-value = 0.032). It is also significantly related to the POPS Father involvement score (p-value = 0.001). The other two dependent variables that it is significantly related to are the POPS Father Autonomy Support (p-value = 0.007) and the PAC Father score (p-value =

0.002). This seems to suggest that depending on the race of the child there is a lot of influence or relationships with the father in the household. As for the gender of the child, there is only one significant relationship and that is between gender and the Introjected Regulation (p-value = 0.029). In order to see where the differences lie with respect to the gender and race of the participants, the parameter estimates for the model are presented in Table 13.

Table 12
MANOVA results for the models that observed significant effects.

Source		Type III Sum of Squares	df	Mean Square	F	Sig.
Intercept	SRQ-A Introjected Regulation	716.308	1	716.308	1398.478	.000
	SRQ-A Relative Autonomy Index (RAI)	15.048	1	15.048	6.302	.013
	POPS Father Involvement	803.451	1	803.451	1862.691	.000
	POPS Father Autonomy Support	519.992	1	519.992	1353.869	.000
	Parent-Adolescent Communication: Father	476283.776	1	476283.776	1859.265	.000
Race	SRQ-A Introjected Regulation	.146	3	.049	.095	.963
	SRQ-A Relative Autonomy Index (RAI)	21.757	3	7.252	3.037	.032
	POPS Father Involvement	8.011	3	2.670	6.191	.001
	POPS Father Autonomy Support	4.931	3	1.644	4.279	.007
	Parent-Adolescent Communication: Father	4132.527	3	1377.509	5.377	.002
Gender	SRQ-A Introjected Regulation	2.499	1	2.499	4.879	.029
	SRQ-A Relative Autonomy Index (RAI)	.072	1	.072	.030	.863
	POPS Father Involvement	.120	1	.120	.277	.599
	POPS Father Autonomy Support	.272	1	.272	.709	.401
	Parent-Adolescent Communication: Father	146.820	1	146.820	.573	.450

Analysis of data show that in the SRQ-A Introjected Regulations that females compared to males would result in a more positive score for this variable since the coefficient is positive and significant. As for the SRQ-A Intrinsic Motivation there is a significant difference in scores for Asian students compared to White students, but overall there wasn't a significant effect on the SRQ-A Intrinsic Motivation score. For the SRQ-A RAI score there is a significant difference between Asian students and White students with Asian students scoring higher than White students because the coefficient is positive.

For the POPS Father Involvement there is a significant difference between Hispanic students and White students (p-value = 0.007). The parameter estimate is negative which illustrates that Hispanic students would score less on the POPS Father Involvement score. As for POPS Father Autonomy Support there is a significant difference between Asian students and White students (p-value = 0.001). The parameter estimate is negative which means that Asian students would score less on the POPS Father Autonomy Support score than White children would. Finally there is a significant difference between Hispanic students and White students with respect to the PAC Father scores (p-value = 0.001). The parameter estimate is negative which illustrates that Hispanic students would score less on the PAC Father scores.

Table 13
Parameter estimates for the results of the MANOVA.

Parameter Estimates

Dependent Variable	Parameter	B	Std. Error	T	Sig.	95% Confidence Interval Lower Bound	Upper Bound
SRQ-A Introjected Regulation	Intercept	2.208	.141	15.660	.000	1.929	2.487
	[race_2=1]	.044	.186	.238	.812	-.324	.412
	[race_2=2]	.069	.174	.397	.692	-.275	.413
	[race_2=3]	.090	.178	.503	.616	-.263	.442
	[race_2=4]	0ª	.	.	.	.	.
	[gender2=1]	.283	.128	2.209	.029	.029	.536
	[gender2=2]	0ª	.	.	.	.	.

Parameter Estimates

Dependent Variable	Parameter	B	Std. Error	T	Sig.	95% Confidence Interval Lower Bound	Upper Bound
SRQ-A Relative	Intercept	-.739	.304	-2.428	.017	-1.342	-.137
Autonomy Index	[race_2=1]	1.142	.402	2.844	.005	.347	1.937
(RAI)	[race_2=2]	.340	.375	.907	.366	-.402	1.082
	[race_2=3]	.179	.384	.466	.642	-.581	.939
	[race_2=4]	0[a]	.	.	.	.	.
	[gender2=1]	-.048	.277	-.173	.863	-.595	.499
	[gender2=2]	0[a]	.	.	.	.	.
POPS Father	Intercept	2.550	.129	19.710	.000	2.294	2.806
Involvement	[race_2=1]	.080	.171	.469	.640	-.258	.418
	[race_2=2]	.213	.159	1.334	.185	-.103	.528
	[race_2=3]	-.449	.163	-2.752	.007	-.772	-.126
	[race_2=4]	0[a]	.	.	.	.	.
	[gender2=1]	.062	.118	.527	.599	-.171	.295
	[gender2=2]	0[a]	.	.	.	.	.
POPS Father	Intercept	2.260	.122	18.515	.000	2.019	2.502
Autonomy	[race_2=1]	-.526	.161	-3.265	.001	-.845	-.207
Support	[race_2=2]	-.069	.150	-.461	.646	-.367	.228
	[race_2=3]	-.080	.154	-.518	.605	-.385	.225
	[race_2=4]	0[a]	.	.	.	.	.
	[gender2=1]	-.093	.111	-.842	.401	-.313	.126
	[gender2=2]	0[a]	.	.	.	.	.
Parent-	Intercept	67.117	3.153	21.288	.000	60.876	73.358
Adolescent	[race_2=1]	-2.536	4.159	-.610	.543	-10.769	5.698
Communication:	[race_2=2]	-.259	3.884	-.067	.947	-7.947	7.429
Father	[race_2=3]	-13.798	3.977	-3.469	.001	-21.672	-5.925
	[race_2=4]	0[a]	.	.	.	.	.
	[gender2=1]	-2.168	2.864	-.757	.450	-7.839	3.502
	[gender2=2]	0[a]	.	.	.	.	.

Summary

It was found in the first assessment of hypothesis one that the variables which had a significant impact on the RAI scores of the students were the POPS mother autonomy group and the PAC father measurement. These two variables together were able to explain approximately 20% of the variation in the RAI scores. This provides evidence against the first null hypothesis, that none of the POPS or PAC scores would have an impact on the RAI scores of the students. In the test of hypothesis 2, it was found that the age and the gender of the student did not have a significant impact on the RAI scores. The total amount of variation that explained by the model increased by 1%, indicated that the age and gender do not contribute to the explanation of the RAI scores. In the test of hypothesis 3, it was found that after fitting an MANOVA to the data, that age and gender had a significant impact on a few of the criterion variables. These variables included the SRQ-A Introjected Regulation, SRQ-A Relative Autonomy Index, POPS Father Involvement, POPS Father Autonomy Support, and the Parent-Adolescent Communication: Father. A discussion of findings is provided in chapter 5 of this study.

CHAPTER 5: SUMMARY, CONCLUSIONS, AND RECOMMENDATIONS

Summary

The purpose of this quantitative study was to explore factors determining adolescents' perceptions of ways they develop autonomy. The theoretical perspective taken in this dissertation is the self-determination theory (SDT). Self-determination emphasizes the concept that autonomy is a basic psychological need for all human beings (Ryan & Deci, 2000). A review of literature showed that adolescents have a strong desire to be self-determined and to do things for themselves. Autonomous behaviors are those that are self-regulated and self- initiated accompanied by a sense of psychological freedom (Craig & Baucum, 2002; Deci & Ryan, 2000). Previous studies have been conducted on parent's beliefs about ways adolescents develop (Rothbaum et al., 2000a). Review of the literature showed adolescents also have opinions and hold personal beliefs (Melton, 2005a). The rationale for this study was that no research has been conducted on adolescents' own beliefs about ways they develop autonomy. Based on these concepts and the results of research, the researcher concluded that parental support and parent adolescent communication are factors that determine adolescents' perceptions of autonomy development.

Conclusion and Discussion of Findings

Three research questions and hypotheses were posted in this study. Following are conclusions regarding those research questions and hypotheses based on data gathered from the RAI of the SRQ-A, the POPS, and the PACS. The RAI of the SRQ-A was used to measure autonomy. The POPS was used to measure perception of parental support. The PACS was used to measure parent adolescent communication.

Research question 1 addressed whether a relationship exists between adolescents' autonomy development and perceptions of parental support and parent adolescent communication.

Null Hypothesis 1: There will be no significant relationship between adolescent's autonomy development and the variables of perception of parental support and parent adolescent communication.

Alternative Hypothesis 1: There is a significant relationship between adolescent's autonomy development and the variables of perception of parental support and parent adolescent communication.

The self-determination theory was the basis of this dissertation. Emphasis was placed on parental support and parent adolescent communication as factors determining adolescents' perceptions of their autonomy development. Based on data presented in chapter 4, there was a correlation between variables. Significant positive relationships were found in relative autonomy (RAI) and perception of parent mother autonomy support (POPS MAS) and parent adolescent communication father (PAC FATH). Results of this study predict that for every unit of increase in Mother Autonomy Support, relative autonomy will also increase. Similarly, for every unit of increase in parent adolescent communication with father, relative autonomy will increase as well. Consistent with other findings (Caprara et al., 1998; Levesque et al., 2004), this study revealed that the more adolescents perceive mothers as supportive, the higher the autonomy. Likewise, the more positive were the beliefs about parent adolescent communication, the greater the autonomy. In this case, parent adolescent communication with fathers was more significantly positively related than parent adolescent communication with mothers. In addition, results of this study showed mothers were more autonomy supportive than fathers. Results of this study reject the Null hypothesis. There is a significant positive relationship between adolescent autonomy development and perception of parental support and parent adolescent communication style.

Research question 2 explored whether adolescents' autonomy development can be predicted by their perceptions of parental support and parent adolescent communication and demographic variables of age and gender.

Null Hypothesis 2: Perceptions of parental support and parent adolescent communication and the demographic variables of age and gender will not each independently account for a significant portion of the variance in autonomy development.

Alternative Hypothesis 2: Perceptions of parental support and parent adolescent communication and the demographic variables of age and gender will each independently account for a significant portion of the variance in autonomy development.

Descriptive statistics presented in chapter 4 showed a higher percentage of females participants (55.4%) than males (44.6 %). In addition, there was a higher percentage of 13 years olds participants (30.8%) followed by 14 year olds (24.6%), with 11 and 12 years old 20% each. There were only six 10-10 ½ year olds (4.6%). Results of preliminary analysis showed all 6 independent variables involving POPS (4) and the PACS (2) measures were found (a) to have at least a significant to bivariate relationship with relative autonomy (RAI SRQ-A) and (b) to have relationships that were linear in nature. Results of regression analysis showed that only 2 of the 8 independent variables showed some evidence in support of hypothesis 2 that autonomy can be predicted to some level of reliability from adolescents' perceptions of parental support. This evidence was revealed in the perception of parental support mother autonomy support (POPS-MAS, p-value =.001) and parent-adolescent communication father (PAC-FATH, p-value =.002). Consistent with other findings (Harter et al., 1998), this study revealed that age and gender did not have a significant effect on relative autonomy. The Null hypothesis was therefore accepted. Perceptions of parental support and parent adolescent communication and the demographic variables of age and gender did not each independently account for a significant portion of variance in autonomy development. Although this study revealed that age and gender did not account for a significant portion of variance in relative autonomy, review of the literature on the self-determination theory indicated that autonomy development is vital for all children (Chirkov & Ryan, 2001).

Research question 3 explored whether there were ethnic group and gender differences in adolescents' autonomy development, perceptions of parental support, and parent adolescent communication?

Null Hypothesis 3: There are no significant differences in beliefs among ethnic groups and by gender of autonomy development, perception of parental support, and parent adolescent communication.

Alternative Hypothesis 3: There are significant differences in beliefs among ethnic groups and by gender of autonomy development, perception of parental support and parent adolescent communication.

The MANOVA was used for this research question to test for a number of different response variables from the same participant and a number of different independent variables at the same time. The independent variables in this case were gender and ethnicity of the adolescent. Asians, Blacks, Hispanics, and Whites were used in this study. From the sample size (n=130), only 127 (n=127) were used in research question 3. Three participants reported Bi-racial demographics. Therefore, Bi-racial subjects were removed from this analysis because a cell of only 3 is not sufficient for calculating a mean score for these individuals.

Results of this study showed that the race of the adolescent has a significant effect on several of the dependent variables. Race was found to be significantly related to the RAI scores (p-value = 0.032). For example, perception of parent father involvement scores for Hispanics were less compared with Asians, Blacks, and Whites. There was also a significant difference in perception of parent father autonomy support between Asians and Whites. Asians scored less than Whites. In addition, there was a significant difference between Hispanics, Blacks, and Whites with respect to parent adolescent communication with father scores. Hispanics scores were less. Results indicated that Hispanics perceived fathers as less involved. Results also indicated Hispanics have a negative perception of communication with fathers. Whites perceived fathers as more autonomy supportive than Asians. This study suggested that depending on the race, there is a lot of influence, both positive and negative, in communication, support, and involvement between adolescents and fathers. As for the gender of the adolescent, results of this study showed there is only one significant relationship and that is between gender and the Introjected Regulation. Females SRQ-A Introjected regulations as compared to males results were more positive and significant suggesting that females are internally motivated by pressures such as self-worth, related contingencies, and feelings of shame and guilt (Ryan & Connell, 1989; Ryan & Deci,2000). Results of this study showed that for the SRQ-A Intrinsic Motivation there was a significant difference in scores for Asians compared to Whites with Asians scoring higher. These results indicated that Asians were more autonomous than Whites. Contrary to findings from other studies on autonomy that external regulation but not identified or intrinsic regulation predict achievement in Taiwan students (d'Ailly, 2003), and Eastern students may thrive when forced to meet expectations (Markus & Kitayama, 2003), results of this study were consistent with the self-determination theory, that is, intrinsically motivated people are self-determined and "engage in an activity for its own sake rather than for the purpose of obtaining an outcome that is separable from the activity itself" (Ryan & Deci, 2000). Results of this study reject the Null hypotheses. There are significant differences in beliefs among ethnic groups and by gender of autonomy development and perceptions of parental support and parent adolescent communication.

Limitations

A number of limitations exist in this study. The population used consisted of a small sample size (*N=130*). For the purpose of this study, participants included a narrow population of middle school students, ages 10-14 and grade level 6th-8th. Ethnic group norms, cultures, and lifestyles may have similarities and overlap between these groups affecting the generalization. This study was limited to a population of ethnic groups including Asians, Blacks, Hispanics, and Whites. Measures or scales other than the ones used in this study may prove as reliable. Caution should be taken when interpreting the results of this study.

During data collection, some participants reported concerns about the number of questions and the questionnaire format. Some participants chose a different method of answering the questions such as turning pages back and forth and working from back to front as opposed to following instructions. A few comments were also made during data collection indicating a desire to answer questions in a socially acceptable manner. Therefore, some questions may not have been answered truthfully. Finally, questions were asked such as why they were participating and whether it was because they volunteered or because they were chosen. This added to the length of time to complete the questionnaires. These factors limit the generalization that can be made from this study.

Implications for Social Change

The present findings have several implications for practice and social change. The implication for social change includes focus on developing programs that contribute to healthy development in all children. Programs should also provide increased awareness and prevention of factors that contribute to adolescents' vulnerability to engage in negative behaviors that potentially lead to juvenile justice is violent and contribute to out of home placement. This study could serve as a tool for professionals and public policy makers to design more culturally sensitive programs that create social change for adolescents and from adolescents' viewpoints.

Implications for public policy makers also include culturally sensitive research taking into account the considerable diversity among ethnic groups. Cultural considerations need to be applied in specific contexts.

Implication for clinicians is to focus on understanding the relationship between individual characteristics of both adolescent and parents. Therapists need to be knowledgeable about various aspects of cultural diversity as it pertains to adolescents, parents, and the family as a whole. More concentration and efforts should be made to understand the complexity of parent-child relationship and behaviors related to risk factors and special needs of the adolescent, parent, and family as a whole. Implications for clinicians also include developing and implementing several techniques and strategies. Some examples are self-monitor thoughts, feelings, and affect, problem solving, and ways to improve communication (Conger et al., 2000; Pinderhughes et al., 2000). In addition, implications for clinicians include self-monitoring of their own comfort zone, ongoing training to increase awareness on culture, ethnicity, and other factors that affect a diverse group of adolescent and families (Smetana et al., 2000). Implication for therapists is to gain the confidence needed to conduct sessions free from bias and personal beliefs. Finally, therapists should incorporate therapeutic techniques that specifically address issues related to autonomy development (d'Ailly, 2003).

Implications for educators include educational programs that teach effective parenting skills, expand knowledge of influences and triggers that effect on parenting (Smetana et al., 2000). Provide programs that teach safe, effective interventions such as coping and communication skills. Prevention and intervention programs would specifically benefit the parent, children all ages, and the entire family. Implication for educators is to design programs to teach and enhance parents' involvement with their adolescents. Implication for teachers would be to examine their role in adolescents' development in the classroom setting.

Implications for communities include efforts to reduce stress and provide networks of support for families. Educating the public about existing and potential problems in the community could serve as proactive tools for adolescents, parents, and families. Another implication is to design programs for families that increase awareness of stressors in the home such as parental demands pertaining to homework, friendships, and curfews (Bradley & Corwyn, 2000).

Implication for families is to examine their roles. Parents can be more alert to the possibility of differential treatment of siblings or gender. Parents need to be aware and conscious of family factors that affect male and female adolescents differently. The role of socialization is another implication and parents may provide and participate in productive extracurricular activities with adolescents to enhance and teach autonomy development. Finally, parents could involve adolescents in family discussions and encourage them to share their ideas and views providing more opportunities for them to develop autonomy (Harter et al, 1998; Melton, 1996).

Recommendations for Action

It is recommended that parents get training on techniques and methods that provide additional insight into factors that contribute to as well as restrict adolescent development. Training should include parental goals such as ways to support and promote growth for adolescents. Parenting skills may also include teaching constructive methods for engaging in self-expressions of personal opinions and overall communication between parents and adolescents. It is recommended that practicing therapists to seek out opportunities to enhance their own knowledge and skills in cultural diversity with particular emphasis on adolescent development.

It is also recommended that therapists incorporate more specific individual and family psychotherapy techniques to meet the needs of addressing autonomy development. This would provide better opportunities for therapists to address the need of the whole individual as well as enhancing the client therapist relationship. In addition, these services could contribute significantly to the profession. These services could also provide a better understanding of how adolescents perceive their parents' role in their development. Findings from this study could serve as a means of bringing attention to the vital need to giving adolescents opportunities to express their views on factors contributing to their autonomy development. Ultimately, this could enhance overall communication between parents and adolescents (Rothbaum et al., 2000). This study could serve as a valuable tool to improving educational and parenting skills for both adolescents and parents. Findings from this study could also contribute significantly to both researcher and practitioners in the areas of services needed to improve parent-child interactions across ethnic groups.

Recommendations for Further Study

It is recommended that this study be done with a larger sample size. Further study should also include a larger geographic location with a more diverse population than one finds in the 6th, 7th, and 8th grade middle school students. In addition, more studies need to be conducted to how important it is to include adolescent viewpoints about ways as they grow and develop. Studies analyzed in this dissertation seemed to indicate such a need especially when one considers autonomy to be a basic human and psychological need (Ryan & Deci, 2000). These applications increase the possibility of better relationships between adolescents and their parents. Further research should compare scales used in this study with other scales such as self-report measures and new scales or measures that may have been developed.

This quantitative study has explored factors determining adolescents' perceptions of their autonomy development. Evidence has been provided to show adolescents' perceptions of parental support and parent adolescent communication styles are factors in developing autonomy.

In conclusion, children, like grown ups, should have the right to decide and have input into matters which affect them most directly. Even though every grown up was once a child and believes he or she knows what it is like to be a child, how quickly they forget. Grown ups become so adsorbed and so serious about what they regard to be the only way to serve the welfare of children, they cease to entertain any other possibilities and fail to see and hear even the children themselves. Grown ups need to ask and seek information from children. However, if grown ups are not willing to listen, they will never truly know what the child has to say. The issue of self determination is at the heart of every child. The UN Convention on the Rights of the Child "establishes the right of a child to be an actor in his or her own development, to express opinions and to have them taken into account in the decisions relating to his or her life" (Melton, 2005b, p. 922). This study provided an opportunity for children to express their views and opinions about their development.

EPILOGUE

Adolescents need parental support to help them develop autonomy. Parents, like every grown up, was once a child and know what it is like to be a child. Yet, how quickly they forget. Grown ups often become so adsorbed and so serious about what they regard to be the only way to serve the welfare of children, they cease to entertain any other possibilities and fail to see and hear even the children themselves. Grown ups can learn by asking and seeking information from children.

ABOUT THE AUTHOR

Gloria D. Fondren, PH.D., is a graduate of Walden University with a Doctorate in Clinical Psychology. She holds a Masters' Degree in Professional Counseling. Dr. Fondren is founder and CEO of Viewpoints for Change, Inc., a non-profit organization and owner of Psychological Services C.A.F. for children, adults, and families. Currently, Dr. Fondren has a private practice in San Antonio, Texas. She is also the author of Praise and Poverty.

REFERENCES

Ackerman, B., Kogos, J., Youngstrom, E., Schoff, K.,& Izard, C. (1999). Family instability and the problem behaviors of children from economically disadvantaged families. *Developmental Psychology, 35*, 258-268.

Adams, P., Berg, L., Berger, N., Duane, M., Neill, A., & Ollendorff, R. (1971). *Children's rights.* New York: Praeger.

Ahmed, K. (2002).Voice and acculturation in relational contexts among South-Asian American college students. *Dissertation Abstracts International Section B: The Sciences and Engineering 62*(7-B), 3416.

Ainsworth, M. (1989). Attachment beyond infancy. *American Psychologist, 44*, 709-716.

Ainsworth, M. & Marvin, R. (1995). On the shaping of attachment theory and research. *Monographs of the Society for Research in Child Development, 60*, 3-24.

Anan, R. & Barnett, D. (1999). Perceived social support mediates prior attachment and subsequent adjustment: A study of urban African American children. *Developmental Psychology, 35*, 1210-1222.

Atkinson, D. R. (2004). *Counseling American minorities: Sixth edition.* NY: McGraw-Hill Companies.

Bandura, A. (1990). *Multidimensional scales of perceived self-efficacy.* Stanford, CA: Stanford University Press.

Bandura, A. (1997*). Self-efficacy: The exercise of control.* New York: W.H. Freeman.

Bandura, A. (2001). Social cognitive theory: An agentic perspective. *Annual Review of Psychology, 52,* 1-26.

Barnes, H. & Olson, D.(1982). Parent-adolescent communication. In D.H. Olson, H.I. McCubbin, H. Barnes, A. Larsen, M. Muxen, & M. Wilson (Eds.), *Family inventories (55-70).* St Paul, MN: University of Minnesota Press.

Baumesiter, R. & Leary, M. (1995). The need to belong: Desire for interpersonal attachments as a function of human motivation. *Psychological Bulletin, 117,* 497-529.

Bhushan, R. & Ravi, A. (1988). Reliability and validity of family functioning and communication scales in Northern India. *Journal of Personality and Clinical Studies, 4,* 227-232.

Blake, S., Simkin, L., Ledsky, R., Perkins, C., & Calabrese, J. (2001). Effects of a parent-child communication intervention on young adolescents' risk for early onset of sexual intercourse. *Family Planning Perspectives, 33,* 52-61.

Boake, C. & Salmon, P. (2006). Demographic correlates and factor structure of the family environment scale. *Journal of Clinical Psychology, 39,* 95-100.

Bohlin, G., Gunilla, R., Hagekull, B., Berit, S., Rydell, A., & Ann-Margret, G. (2000). Attachment and social functioning: A longitudinal study from infancy to middle childhood. *Social Development, 9,* 24-39.

Bohlin, G., Hagekull, B., & Anderson, K. (2005). Behavior inhibition as a precursor of peer social competence in early school age: The interplay with attachment and nonparental care. *Developmental Psychology, 51,* 588-597.

Bowen, M. (1988). *Family evaluation: An approach based on Bowen theory.* Canada: Penguin Books Canada Ltd.

Bowlby, J. (1982). *Attachment and loss, Vol. I. Attachment.* New York: Basic Books.

Bowlby, J. (1989). *Secure attachment.* New York: Basic Books.

Bradley, R. & Corwyn, R. (2000). Moderating effect of perceived amount of family conflict on the relation between home environmental processes and the well-being of adolescents. *Journal of Family Psychology, 14,* 349-364.

Braine, L., Pomerantz, E., Lorber, D., & Krantz, D. (1997). Conflicts with authority: Children's feelings, actions, and justifications. *Developmental Psychology, 27,* 829-840.

Brannen, J. (2002). The use of video in research dissemination: Children as experts on their own family lives. *International Journal of Social Research Methodology: Theory and Practice, 5,* 173-180.

Braungart-Rieker, J. Garwood, M., Powers, B., & Notaro, P. (1999). Infant affect and affect regulation during the still face paradigm with mothers and fathers: The role of infant characteristics and parental sensitivity. *Developmental Psychology, 34,* 1428-1437.

Bronfenbrenner, U. (1995). Developmental ecology through space and time. In P. Moen, G.H. Elder, & K. Luscher (Eds.), *Examining lives in context* (pp. 619-648). Washington, DC: American Psychological Association.

Bronfenbrenner, U. & Morris, P. (1998). *The ecology of the family as a context of human development.* New York: Wiley Press.

Brown, K. & Ryan, R. (2007). Multilevel modeling of motivation: A self-determination theory analysis of basic psychological needs. *Oxford handbook of methods in positive psychology.* Boston: Oxford University Press.

Buddin, B. (1999). The effect of parental expression of opinions and parental support for adolescent voice on the expression of adolescent voice with mother and father. *Dissertation Abstracts International: Section B: The Sciences and Engineering. 59* (8-B), 4506.

Bufe, G. (1997). A study of opinions of children about mental illness and associated predictor variables. *Dissertation Abstracts International: Section B: The Sciences and Engineering. 58*(1-B), 0133.

Bumpus, M., Crouter, A., & McHale, S. (2001). Parental autonomy granting adolescence exploring gender differences in context. *Developmental Psychology, 37,* 163-173.

Butzel, J. & Ryan, R. (1997). The dynamics of volitional reliance. A motivational perspective on dependence, independence, and social support. In G.R. Pierce, B. Lakey, I.G. Sarason, & B.R. Sarason (Eds.), *Sourcebook of social support and personality* (pp. 49-67). New York: Plenum Press.

Camras, L., Chen, Y., Bakeman, R., Norris, K., & Cain, T. (2006). Culture, ethnicity, and children's facial expressions: A study of European American, mainland Chinese, Chinese American, and adopted Chinese girls. *Emotion, 6,* 103-114.

Caprara, G., Regalia, C., & Bandura, A. (2002). Longitudinal impact of perceived self-regulatory efficacy on violent conduct. *European Psychologist, 7,* 63-69.

Caprara, G., Regalia, C., Scabini, E., Barbarnelli, C., & Bandura, A. (2004). Assessment of filial, parental, marital, and collective family efficacy beliefs. *European Journal of Psychological Assessment, 20,* 247-261.

Caprara, G., Scabini, E., Barnarnelli, C., Pastorelli, C., Regalia, C., & Bandura, A. (1998). Impact of adolescents' perceived self-regulatory efficacy on familial communication and antisocial conduct. *European Psychologist, 3,* 125-132.

Carver, R. (2006). *Doing data analysis with SPSS: Version 14.0.* NY: Psychology Press.

Chao, R. (1994). Beyond parental control and authoritarian parenting style: Understanding Chinese parenting through cultural notion of training. *Child Development, 65,* 1111-1119.

Chapman, M., Wall, A., & Barth, R. (2004). Children's voices: The perception of children in foster care. *American Journal of Orthopsychiatry, 74,* 293-304.

Chen, X., Liu, M., & Li, D. (2000). Parental warmth, control, and indulgence and their relations to adjustment in Chinese children: A longitudinal study. *Journal of Family Psychology, 14,* 401-419.

Chirkov, V. & Ryan, R. (2001). Parent and teacher autonomy support in Russian and U.S. adolescents: Common effects on well being and academic motivation. *Journal of Cross-Cultural Psychology, 32,* 681-635.

Chirkov, V., Ryan, R., Kim, Y., & Kaplan, U. (2003). Differentiating autonomy from individualism and independence: A self-determination theory perspective on internalization of cultural orientation and well being. *Journal of Personality and Social Psychology, 84,* 97-110.

Cohen, J. (1992). *Statistical power analysis for behavioral sciences.* Hillsdale, NJ: Erlbaum.

Choo, O. (2002). Parenting behaviors and adolescent psychosocial adjustment: *Gender Differences and Ethnicity Issues in an Asian Context, 17,* 2-7

Chu, H. (2007). Autonomy and well being: Self determination in Chinese students in the United States. *Dissertation Abstracts International: Section B: The Sciences and Engineering. 67(8-B)*, 4702.

Chung, H. & Steinberg, L. (2006). Relations between neighborhood factors, parenting behaviors, peer deviance, and delinquency among serious juvenile offenders. *Developmental Psychology, 42*, 319-331.

Clark, K. & Ladd, G. (2000). Connectedness and autonomy support in parent-child relationships: Links to children's socioemotional orientation and peer relationships. *Developmental Psychology, 36*, 485-498.

Coles, R. (1986). *The moral life of children*. New York, NY: Atlantic Monthly Press.

Coles, R. (1990). *The inner lives of children: The spiritual life of children*. Boston, MA: Houghton Mifflin Company.

Cook, W. (1993). Interdependence and the interdependence sense of control: An analysis of family relationships. *Journal of Personality and Social Psychology, 64*, 587-601.

Conger, R., Ge, X., Elder, G., Lorenz, F., & Simons, R. (1994). Economic stress, coercive family process, and developmental problems in adolescents. *Child Development, 65*, 541-561.

Craig, G. & Baucum, D. (2002). *Human development: Ninth edition*. Upper Saddle River, NJ: Prentice Hall.

Cummings, E., Davies, P., & Campbell, S. (2006). Maladaptation in young children is commonly rooted in experience with family discord. *Developmental Psychopathology and Family relation: Theory, research, and clinical implications*. New York, Guilford Press.

d'Ailly, H. (2003). Children's autonomy and perceived control in learning: A model of motivation and achievement in Taiwan. *Journal of Educational Psychology, 95*, 84-96.

Damon, W. (1990). *The moral child: Nurturing children's natural moral growth*. New York, NY: The Free Press

Davolos, D., Chavez, E., & Guardiola, R. (2005). Effects of perceived parental school support and family communication on delinquent behaviors in Latinos and White non-Latinos. *Cultural Diversity and Ethnic Minority Psychology, 11,* 57-68.

Deci, E. & Ryan, R. (1987). The support of autonomy and the control of behavior. *Journal of Personality and Social Psychology, 53,* 1024-1037.

Deci, E. & Ryan, R. (1995). Human anatomy: The basis for true self esteem. *In M.H. Kernis (Ed.). Efficacy, agency, and self-esteem (pp. 31-46).* New York: Plenum Press.

Dilts, R.B. (1999). *Sleigh of mouth: The magic of conversational belief change.* Capitola, CA: Meta Publications.

Dodge, K., Pettit, G., & Bates, J. (2000). Socialization mediators of the relation between socioeconomic status and child conduct problems. *Child Development, 65,* 649-665.

Duncan, G. & Brooks-Gunn, J. (1997). Income effects across the life span; Integration and interpretation. In G.J. Duncan & J. Brooks-Gunn (Eds.), *Consequences of growing up poor* (pp. 596-610). New York; Russell Sage Foundation.

Dweck, C. & Kaminis, S. (1999). *Self theories: Their role in motivation, personality, and development.* Philadelphia: Taylor and Francis Psychology Press.

Eccles, J., Early, D., Frasier, K., Belansky, E., & McCarthy, K. (1996). The relation of connection, regulation, and support for autonomy to adolescents' functioning. *Journal of Adolescent Research, 12,* 263-286.

Eisenberg, N., Gershoff, E., Fabes, R., Shepard, S., Cumberland, A., Losoya, S., Guthrie, I., & Murphy, B. (2001). Mother's emotional expressivity and children's behavior problems and social competence: mediation through children's regulation. (2001). *Developmental Psychology, 37,* 475-490.

Erikson, E. (1980). *Identity, youth, and life crisis.* New York: Norton & Company, Inc.

Erikson, E. (1982). *The life cycle completed.* New York: Rikan Enterprises Ltd.

Fincham, F., Beach, S., Arias, I., & Brody, G. (1998). Children's attributions in the family: *The Children's Relationship Attribution Measure, 12,* 481-493.

Florsheim, P., Tolan, P., & Gorman-Smith, D. (1996). Family process and risk for externalizing behavior problems among African American and Hispanic boys. *Journal of Consulting and Clinical Psychology, 64,* 1222-1230.

Fosco, G. & Grych, J. (2007). Emotional expression in the family as a context for children's appraisals of interparental conflict. *Journal of Family Psychology, 21,* 248-258.

Garth, B. & Aroni, R. (2003). I value what you have to say: Seeking the perspective of children with a disability, not just their parents. *Disability and Society, 18,* 561-576.

Garbarino, J. & Scott, F. (1992). *What children can tell us: Eliciting, interpreting, and evaluating critical information from children.* San Francisco, CA: Jossey-Bass Publishers.

Garbarino, J. (1995). The American war zone: What children can tell us about living with violence. *Journal of Development and Behavioral Pediatrics, 16,* 431-435.

Gilligan, C. (1982). *In a different voice.* Cambridge, MA: Harvard University Press.

Gilligan, C. (1993). Joining the resistance: Psychology, politics, girls, and women. In L. Weis & M. Fine (Eds.), *Beyond silenced voices* (pp. 143-168). Albany: State University of New York Press.

Ginsberg, H.P. (1997).*Entering the child's mind: The clinical interview in psychological research and practice.* New York: Cambridge University Press.

Goldberg, S., Grusec, J., & Jenkins, J. (1999). Confidence in Protection: Arguments for a narrow definition of attachment. *Journal of Family Psychology, 13,* 475-483.

Gonzales, N., Pitts, S., Hill, N., & Roosa, M. (2000). A mediational model of the impact of interparental conflict on child adjustment in a multiethnic, low income sample. *Journal of Family Psychology, 14,* 365-379.

Gorman-Smith, D., Tolan, P., Henry, D., Florsheim, P. (2000). Patterns of family functioning and adolescent outcomes among urban African American and Mexican American families. *Journal of Family Psychology, 14,* 436-457.

Gralinski J. & Kopp, C. (1993). Everyday rules for behavior: Mothers' requests to young children. *Developmental Psychology, 29,* 573-584.

Grolnick, W., Benjet, C., Kurowski, C., & Apostoleris, N. (1997). Predictors of parent involvement in children' schooling. *Journal of Educational Psychology, 89,* 538-548.

Grolnick, W., Deci, E., & Ryan, R. (1997). Internalization within the Family: The self-determination theory perspective. *Journal of Personality and Social Psychology, 34,* 393-404.

Grolnick, W. & Ryan, R. (1987). Autonomy in children's learning: An experimental and individual difference investigation. *Journal of Personality and Social Psychology, 52,* 890-898.

Grolnick, W., Ryan, R., & Deci, E. (1991). Inner resources for school achievement: Motivational mediators of children's perception of their parents. *Journal of Educational Psychology, 83,* 508-517.

Grotevant, H. & Cooper, C. (1998). Individuation in family relationships: A perspective on individual differences in the development of identity and role-taking skill in adolescence. *Human Development, 29(2),* 82-100.

Guay, F., Senecal, C., Guathier, L., & Forrest, C. (2003). Predicting career indecision: A self-determination theory perspective. *Journal of Counseling Psychology, 50,* 165-177.

Hallstrom, I. (2004). The parents' and children's involvement in decision-making during hospitalization. *American Psychologist, 4,* 263-269.

Hand, D.J., & Taylor, C.C. (1987). *Multivariate analysis of variance and repeated measures: A practical approach for behavioral sciencists.* New York: Chapham & Hall.

Hans, M. Weisz, R., & Mesman, J. (2001). Early preschool predictors of preadolescent internalizing and externalizing DSM-IV Diagnoses. *Journal of the American Academy of Child and Adolescent Psychiatry, 40,* 1029-1036.

Hart, S. (1991a). Children's rights in education: An historical perspective. *School Psychology Review, 20,* 345-358.

Hart, S. (1991b). From property to person status: Historical perspective on children's rights. *American Psychologist, 46,* 53-59.

Harter, S. (1990). Issues in the assessment of the self-concept of children and adolescents. In A. LaGreca (Ed.), *Through the eyes of a child* (pp. 292-325). Boston: Allyn & Bacon.

Harter, S. (1998). The development of self-representations. In W. Damon (Series Ed.) & N. Eisenberg (Vol. Ed.), *Handbook of child psychology:*

Vol. 3, Social, emotional, and personality development (5ᵗʰ ed., pp. 553-617). New York: Wiley.

Harter, S., Waters, P., Whitesell, N., & Kastelic, D. (1998). Level of voice among female and male high school students: Relational context, support, and gender orientation. *Developmental Psychology, 34,* 892-901.

Herzig, L. (2006). The meaning (s) of a menopausal woman's voice. *Dissertation Abstracts International Section A: Humanities and Social Sciences.* 67(5-A), 2006, 1947.

Hoff-Ginsberg, E. & Tardif, T. (1995). *Socioeconomic status and parenting. In M. H. Bornstein (Ed.), Children and parenting (Vol.2).* Hillsdale, NJ: Erlbaum.

Hojat, M. (1997). The U.N. Convention on the Rights of the Child: Lost in the class of adverse opinions. *American Psychologist, 52,* 1384-1385.

Jacobs, J., Bleeker, M., & Constantino, M. (2003). The self-system during childhood and adolescence: Development, influences, and implications. *Journal of Psychotherapy Integration, 13,* 33-65.

Johnson, V. (2003). Linking changes in whole family functioning and children's externalizing behavior across the elementary school years. *Journal of Family Psychology, 17,* 499-509.

Jones, C. & Meredith, W. (1996). Patterns of personality and change across the life span. *Psychology and Aging, 11,* 57-65.

Keener, D. & Boykin, K. (1996). Parental control, autonomy, and ego development. *Paper presented at the meeting of the Society for research on Adolescence*, Boston.

Kim, S. & Ge, X. (2000). Parenting practices and adolescent depressive symptoms in Chinese American families. *Journal of Family Psychology, 14,* 420-453.

Kittmer, M. (2005). Risk and resilence in alcoholic families: Family functioning, sibling attachment, and parent-child relationships. *Dissertation Abstracts International: Section B. The Sciences and Engineering.* 65 (8-B), 4339.

Kochanska, G. (2002). Committed compliance, moral self, and internalization: A mediational model. *Developmental Psychology, 38,* 339-351.

Kowal, A., Kramer, L., Krull, J., & Crick, N. (2002). Children's perceptions of the fairness of parental preferential treatment and their socioemotional well being. *Journal of Family Psychology, 16,* 297-306.

Krebs, D & Denton, K. (2006). Explanatory limitations of cognitive-developmental approache's to morality. *Psychological Review, 113,* 672-675.

Landry, S., Smith, K., & Swank, P. (2006). Responsive parenting: Establishing early foundations for social, communication, and independent problem-solving skills. *Developmental Psychology, 42,* 627-642.

Lee, R., Choe, J., Kim, G., & Ngo, V. (2000). Construction of the Asian American family conflicts scale. *Journal of Counseling Psychology, 47,* 211-222.

Lefkowitz, E., Romo, L., Corona, R., Kit-fong Au, T., & Sigman. (2000). How Latino American and European American adolescents discuss conflicts, sexuality, and AIDS with their mother. *Developmental Psychology, 47,* 315-325.

Levesque, C., Zuehlke, A., Stanek, L., & Ryan, R. (2004). Autonomy and competence in German and American university students: A comparative study based on SDT. *Journal of Educational Psychology, 96,* 68-84.

Levine, L., Stein, N., & Liwag, M. (1999). Remembering children's emotions: Sources of concordant and discordant accounts between parents and children. *Developmental Psychology, 35,* 790-801.

Linver, M., Brooks-Gunn, J., & Kohler, D. (2002). *Do maternal parenting and emotional distress mediate association between income and young children's development?* New York: Columbia University Press.

Low, S. & Stocker, C. (2002). Family functioning and children's adjustment: Associations among parent's depressed mood, marital hostility, parent-child hostility, and children's adjustment. *Journal of Family Psychology, 19*, 394-403.

Mandara, J. & Murray, C. (2000). Effects of parental marital status, income, and family functioning on African American adolescent self-esteem. *Journal ofFfamily Psychology, 14*, 475-490.

McLoyd, V. (1998). Socioeconomic disadvantage and child development. *American Psychologist, 53*, 185-204.

McLoyd, V., Kaplan, R., Hardaway, C., & Wood, D. (2007). Does endorsement of physical discipline matter? Assessing moderating influences on the maternal and child psychological correlates of physical discipline in African American families. *Journal of Family Psychology, 21*, 165-174.

Measelle, J., John, O., Ablow, J., Cowan, P., & Cowan, C. (2005). Can children provide coherent, stable, and valid self reports on the Big Five Dimension? A longitudinal study from ages 5 to 7. *Journal of Educational Psychology, 97*, 468-483.

Melton, G. (1991a). Preserving the dignity of children around the world: *The U.N. Convention on the Rights of the Child. Child Abuse and Neglect, 15*, 343-350.

Melton, G. (1991b). Socialization in the global community: Respect for the dignity of children. *American Psychologist, 46*, 66-71.

Melton, G. (1996). The child's right to a family environment: Why children's rights and family values are compatible. *American Psychologist, 51*, 1234-1238.

Melton, G. (2005a). Treating children like people: A framework for research and advocacy. *Journal of Clinical Child and Adolescent Psychology, 34,* 646-657.

Melton, G. (2005b). Building humane communities respectful of children: The significance of the Convention on the Rights of the Child. *American Psychologist, 60,* 918-926.

Minuchin, P. (1985). Families and individual development: Provocations from the field of family therapy. *Child Development, 56,* 289-302.

Moore, D. S., & McCabe, G.P. (2004). Introduction to the practice of statistics. New York: W. H. Freeman & Co.

Moore, P., Whaley, S., & Sigman, M. (2004). Interactions between mothers and children: Impacts of maternal and child anxiety. *Journal of Abnormal Psychology, 113,* 471-476.

Moos, R. & Moos, B. (1990). *Family environment manual: development, applications, research.* Palo Alto, CA: Consulting Psychologist Press.

Morreale, S., Osborn, M. & Pearson, J. (2000). Why communication is important: A rationale for the centrality of the study of communication. *Journal of Association for Communication Administration, 29* (1), 1-25.

Moss, E., Cyr, C., & Dubois-Comtois. (2004). Attachment at early school age and developmental risk: Examining family contexts and behavior problems of controlling-caregiving, controlling-punitive, and behaviorally disorganized children. *Developmental Psychology, 40,* 591-532.

Murphy-Berman, V., levesque, L. & Weisz, V. (1996). U.N. Convention on the Rights of the Child: Current challenges. *American Psychologist, 51,* 1254-1260.

Negy, C. & Snyder, D. (2006). Assessing family of origin functioning in Mexican American adults: retrospective application of the Family Environment Scale. *Assessment, 13,* 396-405.

Neiderhiser, J., Pike, A., Hetherington, E., & Reiss, D. (1998). Adolescent perceptions as mediatiors of parenting: Genetic environmental contributors. *Developmental Psychology, 34,* 1459-1469.

Neitzel, C. & Stright, A. (2003). Mother's scaffolding of children's problem solving" establishing a foundation of academic self-regulatory competence. *Journal of Family Psychology, 17,* 147-159.

Ngo, P. & Malz, A. (1998). Cross-cultural and cross-generational differences in African Americans' cultural and familial systems and their impact on academic striving. In H. McCubbin, E.A. Thompson, A. I. Thompson, & J.E. Fromer (Eds.), *Resilency in Native American and immigrant families* (pp. 265-274). Thousand Oaks, CA: Sage.

Nichols, M. (2005). Stop arguing with your kids: How to win the battle of wills by making children feel heard. *Families, Systems, & Health, 23,* 239-241.

Okazaki, S. (1997). Sources of ethnic differences between Asian American and White American college students on measures of depression and social anxiety. *Journal of Abnormal Psychology, 106,* 52-60.

Parke, R.D. (2000). Beyond White and middle class: Cultural variations in families assessments, processes, and policies. *Journal of Family Psychology, 14,* 331-333.

Parke, R. & Buriel, R. (1998). Socialization in the family: Ethnic and ecological perspectives. In W. Damon & N. Eisenberg (Eds.) *Handbook of child psychology: Social, emotional, and personality development* (5th ed., pp. 463-552). New York: Wiley.

Patrick, H., Canevello, A., Knee, C., & Lonsbary, C. (2007). The role of need fulfillment in relationship functioning and well being: A self-determination theory perspective. *Journal of Personality and Social Psychology, 3,* 434-457.

Patrick, B., Skinner, E., & Cornell, J. (1993). What motivates children's behavior and emotion? Joint effects of perceived control and autonomy in the academic domain. *Journal of Personality and Social Psychology, 65,* 781-791.

Pedersen, S. & Revenson, T. (2005). Parental illness, family functioning, and adolescent well-being: A family ecology framework to guide research. *Journal of Family Psychology, 19,* 404-419.

Petrocelli, J. (2003a). Hierarchical multiple regression in counseling research: Common problems and possible remedies. *Measurement and Evaluation in Counseling and Development, 36,* 9-22.

Petrocelli, J. (2003b). The role of general family functioning in the quality of the mother-daughter relationship of female African American juvenile offenders. *Journal of Black Psychology, 29,* 378-392.

Pettit, G., Keliey, M., Laird, R., Bates, J., & Dodge, K. (2007). Predicting the developmental course of mother-reported monitoring across childhood and adolescence from early proactive parenting, child temperament, and parents' worries. *Journal of Family Psychology, 21,* 206-217.

Piaget, J. (1965). *Moral judgment of children.* New York: Free Press.

Piaget, J. (1966). *Judgment and reasoning in the child.* New York: Notre Press

Pinderhughes, E., Dodge, K., Bates, J., Pettit, G., & Zelli, A. (2000). Discipline responses: Influences of parents' socioeconomic status, ethnicity, beliefs about parenting, stress, and cognitive-emotional processes. *Journal of Family Psychology, 14,* 380-400.

Polit, D. & Hungler, B. (1999). *Accompany nursing research: Principles and methods.* Storrs, CT: Lippincott. Williams & Wilkin Publishers

Querido, J., Warner, T., & Eyberg, S. (2002). Parenting styles and child behavior in African American families of preschool children. *Journal of Clinical Child and Adolescent Psychology, 31,* 272-277.

Rogers, C. (1989). *On becoming a person.* New York: Houghton Mifflin Company.

Rothbaum, F., Morelli, G., Pott, M., & Liu-Constant, Y. (2000a). Immigrant-Chinese and Euro-American parents' physical closeness with young children: Themes of family relatedness. *Journal of Family Psychology, 14,* 334-348.

Rothbaum, F., Weisz, J., Pott, M., Miyake, K., & Morelli, G. (2000b). Attachment and culture security in the United States and Japan. American Psychologist, 55, 1093-1104.

Ryan, R. & Deci, E. (2000). SDT and the facilitation of intrinsic motivation, social development, and well being. *American Psychologist, 55,* 68-78.

Ryan, R. Kuhl, L., & Deci, E. (1992). *Intrinsic motivation and self determination in human behavior.* New York: Plenum.

Sales, J., Milhausen, R., Wingood, G., DiClemente, R., Salazar, L., & Crosby, R. (2006). Validation of a Parent-Adolescent Communication Scale for use in STD/HIV prevention interventions. *Health Education & Behavior, 10,* 1-14.

Santrock, J. (1999). *Life span development: Seventh edition.* Boston, MA: McGraw-Hill.

Satir, V. (1988). *The new peoplemaking.* Palo Alto, CA: Science and Behavior Books, Inc.

Satir, V. (1994). *Helping families change.* Palo Alto, CA: Science and behavior Books, Inc.

Satir, V. & Whitaker, C. (2000). *Experiential approach to family therapy.* Palo Alto, CA: Science and Behavior Books, Inc.

Scabini, E., Lanz, M., & Marta, E. (1999). Psycho-social adjustment and family relationships: A typology of Italian families with a late adolescent. *Journal of Youth and Adolescence, 28,* 633-644.

Scarr, S. (1996). Best of human genetics. *Contemporary Psychology, 41,* 149-150.

Shafer, C. & Gordon, L. (1995). *How to talk to teens about really important things: Specific questions and answers and useful things to say.* San Francisco: Jossey-Bass, Inc.

Silk, J., Morris, A., Kanaga, T., & Steinberg, L., (2003). Psychological control and autonomy granting: Opposite ends of a continuum or distinct constructs. *Journal of Research and Adolescence, 13,* 113-128.

Singer, L. & Weinstein, R. (2000). Differential parental treatment predicts achievement and self-perceptions in two cultural contexts. *Journal of Family Psychology, 14,* 491-509.

Skowron, E. (2005). Parent differentiation of self and child competence in low-income urban families. *Journal of Counseling Psychology, 53,* 337-346.

Smetana, J., Abernathy, A., & Harris, A. (2000). Adolescent-parent interactions in middle-class African American families: Longitudinal change and contextual variations. *Journal of Family Psychology, 14,* 458-474.

Soenens, B., Vansteenkiste, M., Luyckx, K., & Goossens, L. (2006). Parenting and adolescent problem behavior: An integrated model with adolescent self-disclosure and perceived parental knowledge as integrating variables. *Developmental Psychology, 42,* 305-318.

Soto, J., Levenson, R., & Ebling, R. (2005). Cultures of moderation and expression: Emotional experience, behavior, and physiology in Chinese Americans and Mexican Americans. *Emotion, 5,* 154-165.

Spencer, M. & Dupree, D. (1996). African American youths' eco-cultural challenges and psychosocial opportunities: An alternative analysis of problem behavior outcome. In D. Cicchetti & S. L. Toth (Eds.), *Adolescence: Opportunities and challenges* (pp. 259-282). Rochester, NY: University of Rochester Press.

Spiegel, M.R. & Stephens, L.J. (1999). *Schaum's outline of statistics.* New York: McGraw-Hill.

Stepp, L. (2000). *Our last best shot. Guiding our children through early adolescence.* New York, NY: Riverhead Books.

Stevenson-Hinde. (1998). Parenting in different cultures: Time to focus. *Developmental Psychology, 34,* 698-700.

Sue, D.W. & Sue, D. (2003). *Counseling the culturally diverse: Theory and practice.* New York: John Wiley & Sons.

Tenebaum, H. & Leaper, C. (2003). Parent-child conversations about science: The socialization of gender inequities. *Developmental Psychology, 39,* 34-47.

Thorkildsen, T., Sodonis, A., & White-McNulty, L. (2004). Epistemology and adolescents' conceptions of procedural justice in school. *Journal of Educational Psychology, 96,* 347-359.

Vansteenkiste, M., Zhou, M., Lens, W., & Soenens, B. (2004). Experiencies of autonomy and control among Chinese learners: Vitalizing of immobilizing. *Child Development, 76,* 483-501.

Whitaker, C. (1992). *The family crucible.* Palo Alto, CA. Science and Behavior Books.

Wills, T., Gibbons, F., Gerrard, M., Murry, V., & Bordy, G. (2003). Family communication and religiosity related to substance use and sexual behavior in early adolescence: A test for pathways through self-control and prototype perceptions. *Psychology of Addictive Behaviors, 17,* 312-323.

Winter, M., Davies, P., Meyer, S., & Hightower, A. (2006). Relations among family discord, caregiver communication, and children's family representation. *Journal of Family Psychology, 20*, 348-351.

Yamamoto, K. (1993). *Their world, our world: Reflections on childhood.* Westport, CT: Praeger Publishers.

Yero, J. L. (2002*). Beliefs: Teaching in Mind.* Hamilton, MT: Mind Flight Publishing.